Praise for *Love Her, Love Her Not*

[Love Her, Love Her Not: The Hillary Paradox] . . . will most please those who share, in the words of Bamberger's introduction, an "endless fascination with all things Hillary.

—*Publishers Weekly*

Whether Hillary Clinton's candidacy for president gives you a flitter of excitement or a pit of dread, these twenty-eight essays in *Love Her, Love Her Not* are an election season must-read. Though each is unique in its point of view and assessment of her, together they remind us why 2016 is going to be a crucial year in our nation's political history. After reading Joanne Bamberger's expertly curated selection, you'll be ready to be a guest on Bill Maher, even if it's just from your couch.

—**Angela Matusik**, Executive Digital Editor, *InStyle*

In *Love Her, Love Her Not*, Joanne Bamberger sets the stage for rethinking what we already know about Hillary Clinton. Bamberger examines the social and political dynamics that brought us to this historic electoral moment and then hands the stage to some of today's best women pundits and writers to answer our biggest question about the woman most of us refer to simply as 'Hillary': Why are we so conflicted about her as with no other politician?

—**Lisa Belkin**, Senior National Correspondent, Yahoo News

Each one of these entertaining and insightful essays made me think in a new way about Hillary Clinton. *Love Her, Love Her Not* is a must-read before the 2016 election.

—**Leslie Sanchez**, political analyst and author of You've Come a Long Way, Maybe: Sarah, Michelle, Hillary, and the Shaping of the New American Woman

Think you know Hillary Clinton? Think again! Just in time for 2016, *Love Her, Love Her Not* is an indispensable guide to the woman who's already put 18 million cracks in the highest, hardest glass ceiling and may be poised to do a whole lot more.

—**Krystal Ball**, former MSNBC host and congressional candidate

Bamberger's *Love Her, Love Her Not* is a book every American should read before casting a ballot in the 2016 presidential election. With precision and skillful editing, Bamberger assembles an influential collection of diverse voices to give us a chorus of smart and sometimes controversial opinions about one of the most important political figures in history. Regardless of the outcome of the election, this book is a winner!

—**Julie Burton**, President, Women's Media Center

Look no further than this collection of smart, witty, and provocative essays by some of today's most interesting women writers to refine what you think about a future Clinton presidency. *Love Her, Love Her Not* is definitely the book to prepare you for all conversations about Hillary as we head to 2016. Thanks, Joanne Bamberger, for bringing us these essential writings.

—**Carol Jenkins**, Emmy-winning journalist and executive producer of the award-winning documentary, What I Want My Words to Do to You

Hillary is an enigma, wrapped in a mystery, stuffed in a conundrum. Or. Maybe she's just a human woman who has somehow become representative of all women trying to break new ground . . . as firsts and pioneers and ground-breakers often and inevitably do. She's a stand-in for our every secret fear, hope, wish, bias, and more . . . projected, reflected, and rarely corrected. I didn't know how many feelings women had about Hillary—hell, I didn't know how many feelings *I* had about Hillary—until I read Joanne Bamberger's anthology, which was far more hilarious and thought-provoking and *surprising* than it has any right to be, given that this is a woman who has been in the public eye for decades now. Instructive, and never reductive, for this upcoming election season.

—**Elisa Camahort Page**, SheKnows Media Senior Vice President and BlogHer Co-founder

Love Her, Love Her Not

Love Her, Love Her Not

THE HILLARY PARADOX

Edited by Joanne Cronrath Bamberger

SHE WRITES PRESS

Published 2015
Printed in the United States of America
ISBN: 978-1-63152-806-4
Library of Congress Control Number: 2015943665

For information, address:
She Writes Press
1563 Solano Ave #546
Berkeley, CA 94707

She Writes Press is a division of SparkPoint Studio, LLC.

For my daughter Rachel, with the hope that we will both see a woman president in our lifetimes

And for my husband David, who encourages me in all things

Also by Joanne Cronrath Bamberger

*Mothers of Intention: How Women & Social
Media Are Revolutionizing Politics in America*
(2011)

CONTENTS

Introduction

Our country has a very complicated relationship with Hillary Clinton.

Some people love her for her fearless advocacy work around the world with women and girls. Some people hate her because they think she's a wicked political opportunist. Some are confused, teetering on the fence, wanting a woman elected president during their lifetimes, but they're just not sure Hillary is "the one." Conspiracy theorists from her husband's days in the White House claim she can't be trusted because there's a complicated joint Clinton plan for each of them to be president. She's been called the "most hated" First Lady by the *New York Times*, but she's been voted the most admired woman in the world seventeen times in Gallup's annual poll. Progressives who should be active in her campaign yearn for another Democrat—any other Democrat—and GOP women are looking for a way to support her without feeling like Republican Benedict Arnolds.

She's "nagging," "conniving," and "controlling." And don't forget "polarizing." She's "fearless," "loyal," and "intelligent." She's a powerful advocate and a thoughtful friend. She's obsessed with power, and she's a selfless champion for others. When it comes to Hillary Clinton, we just can't seem to make up our minds about whether we admire her for all the things she's accomplished or whether we detest her because she's a woman who's not afraid to admit her own ambitions for political power.

Hillary even started getting criticism from both sides of the political fence, minutes after she announced her 2016 candidacy for president, on the details of how and when it happened: Why was it a video? Why not a live event announcement? Why was it three hours later than expected? Why didn't she mention foreign policy? Is she pushing the "estrogen factor" too hard?

Our endless fascination with all things Hillary gives her a national profile most other politicians can only dream of: the Wellesley graduate, the law firm partner, the First Lady, the senator, the presidential candidate, the global diplomat. And, of course, there are the Hillary distractions—the pantsuits, the nutcracker, the hairstyles, the vanishing emails—that most White House hopefuls are glad they'll never have to worry about. There is no doubt that when it comes to the range of emotions Americans feel about Hillary, she is in a category all her own; she is on the receiving end of a visceral level of love and hate that transcends that of almost all her potential opponents.

But why? How have we become so conflicted over one woman with the kind of goals and ambitions that most of us would encourage in our own mothers or daughters?

Her polling resembles a wild roller coaster ride. During her husband's impeachment, she received the highest of her polling numbers, and the lowest of the lows came during her first campaign for the White House. Hillary's social media presence reflects those extremes, as well. Search the term "Hillary Clinton haters" on the Internet, and you get roughly three million results; try "Hillary Clinton lovers," and you end up with close to four million hits. Over four million people follow her on Twitter, and numerous Facebook pages dedicated to her supporters and detractors boast almost three million fans, not counting the personal Facebook page she created immediately after the official announcement of her campaign in April 2015. Sellers at the craft site Etsy hawk myriad products devoted to her, and Hillary's face graces plenty of boards, both pro and con, on Pinterest.

Love. Hate. Obsession. Devotion. Hostility. Loyalty. Given the various conflicting emotions Hillary Clinton brings out in so many of us, one has to wonder whether our Hillary obsession deserves its own therapeutic diagnostic code.

Poor Hillary.

Growing up in 1950s middle America, Hillary Rodham, as she was known then, dreamt of a career with NASA. By the 1970s, she had tossed the astronaut fantasies to the side, and with a Seven Sisters college education, she entered the world of law and politics. But could she have imagined that in her AARP years, that the little girl from Illinois would be one of the most adored—and reviled—women in the world?

To paraphrase Yoda, the force is strong in those who are both for and against Hillary.

Having mixed feelings about a presidential candidate is nothing new. Many voters are often torn about their potential leaders, and that's exactly where Hillary's political foes want voters to be—straddling that fence between love and hate. In that regard, fomenting mistrust about one's opposition isn't just "a Clinton thing." Many Democrats, who were likely Hillary supporters, fell in love with Barack Obama and his "Yes We Can" theme of 2008. While Hillary ran a fierce primary campaign against him, he faced an even bigger battle during the general election when some extreme right-wing Republicans wanted voters to believe Obama was born in Kenya and therefore not eligible to be president. It's also not just a Democratic thing. During George W. Bush's campaigns, either voters wanted to have a beer with the guy or thought he should be impeached for using the events of September 11, 2001, as an excuse to invade Iraq.

One thing is safe to say—no American politician who has run for president has survived the media and voter hostility that Hillary Rodham Clinton has. She is clearly in a category all her own. But as voters, there are four Hillary groups Americans fall into: lovers, haters, those who hate to love her, and those who love to hate her.

Hillary Clinton is the most politically accomplished woman in America, so much so that she is often referred to and known by one name: Hillary—like Madonna or Bono—that's how much of a rock star she is. Yet, because she is a fearless woman who earned her political stripes during the "I Am Woman" 1970s, she has been on the receiving end of gendered vitriol more times than not. A full list of the sexist mockery she's endured over the last three decades would take up much of this book! Some of the more infamous slams include "Rhymes with rich," "Make me a sandwich!" and "Iron my shirt!" Anytime Hillary does anything—good or bad—she becomes, unfairly, a joke. She was even skewered by jabs claiming that she faked a concussion to avoid congressional testimony—"Help, I've fallen and I can't testify about Benghazi!" And just at a time when she thought it was safe to start dipping her toe in public appearances before her White House run, she was hit with a "scandal" about her private email server during her secretary of state days, bringing cries that she had "possibly" acted illegally. *What could she be hiding?! Oh, there goes that Clinton penchant for secrecy again!* Only to have reporters conclude after a lengthy media firestorm that others before her had done the same thing with official emails, that no laws had been broken, and that media speculation for the sake of headlines does not a campaign-ending scandal make.

Her personal life is certainly not off-limits and has provided plenty of fodder for both her political foes and the media. She's been accused of staying married to Bill after many reported sexual peccadillos, not out of any sense of loyalty, love, or commitment to their marriage, but merely to more smoothly pave the way for her own presidential ambitions. While Monica Lewinsky has become something of a reinvention heroine after her TED talk on bullying, Hillary, as the wronged wife, is still the one who is most harshly judged. Many women believe that's a disqualifier for the presidency, even though voters have, for the most part, forgiven her husband.

And not to be left out, a cottage industry of sorts has grown up around the lucrative market in Hillary hate, with Amazon titles like *Hillary's Scheme: Inside the Next Clinton's Ruthless Agenda to Take the White House* and *Can She Be Stopped: Hillary Clinton Will Be the Next President of the United States Unless* . . . . Misogyny and the general distaste surrounding Hillary have become such phenomena that a developing field of academic study explores the hatred that passes for political commentary and analysis about her. University professors have penned articles with titles like "Rhymes with Blunt: Pornification and U.S. Political Culture," "Texts (and Tweets) from Hillary: Meta-Meming and Postfeminist Political Culture," and "Is She Attractive Enough?" And with a crop of academic books about Hillary, like *Hillary Clinton in the News: Gender and Authenticity in American Politics* and *Woman President: Confronting Postfeminist Political Culture,* can a college-level course in "Hillary Studies" be far off?

The media jabs about her age and looks, which gave rise to those academic explorations, aren't going away. The focus on her age in the days since she left the State Department is back with the same vengeance as in 2008, evidenced by headlines like "Affluent Grandmother is 2016 Frontrunner," while others suggest that the grandmotherly Hillary, along with her daughter Chelsea, could be a 2016 mother/daughter secret campaign weapon. Even President Obama, who ought to be her ally after all the support she and Bill Clinton gave to his campaigns, made a not-so-subtle poke at her advancing age in early 2015, suggesting that in the next presidential election voters are going to want a candidate with a "new car smell." The good news is that if her critics' concerns over her age are carried to their logical conclusion, a post-menopausal Hillary will at least be awake for that infamous 3 a.m. phone call, whether it be from hot flashes or age-related insomnia.

So where is the love?

While it's sometimes less evident in the media, there is plenty of devotion among ardent supporters. That adoration may not receive the same media attention as her haters' venom, but her fans' fervor is equally strong. The Ready for Hillary Super PAC (which changed its name, for legal reasons, to 'ReadyPAC' after she announced the official start of her campaign) was launched in 2013 to keep grass-roots interest and fundraising for a 2016 run alive. Ready for Hillary raised well over $13 million, mostly in small contributions, with the help of "The Hillary Bus" that toured the country to reach out to her fans, as well as with plenty of Hillary swag that was available for sale, including bumper stickers, T-shirts, and pet attire!

High-profile supporters like feminist Gloria Steinem contended in 2008 that Hillary was much more qualified than Barack Obama to become president, noting that if Obama had been a woman with the same resume, "she" would have been skewered over her lack of qualifications. Hillary is worshipped in pop culture memes like her "BFF selfies" with Meryl Streep at the Kennedy Center Honors gala and the humorous "Texts from Hillary," the now famous Tumblr site highlighting then Secretary of State Clinton with her badass shades and Blackberry, looking as if she were already running the world from her official government plane while others, including President Obama and Vice President Joe Biden, vied haplessly for her attention.

And, of course, one of the most famous media tributes to Hillary flipped the hate on its head. "Bitch is the New Black," a phrase coined by Tina Fey and Amy Poehler on *Saturday Night Live*, turned one of the most used slurs against Hillary into a stunning positive:

> *People say Hillary is a bitch . . . Yeah. She is. And so am I . . . You know what. Bitches get stuff done!*

Ultimately, Hillary's Twitter bio, unlike anyone else's on the planet, just may say it all: "Wife, mom, grandma, women+kids advocate, FLOTUS, Senator, SecState, hair icon, pantsuit aficionado, 2016 presidential candidate . . ." That's enough to cause jealousy in all camps, right? Sadly, when she updated that bio after officially declaring her candidacy, "glass ceiling cracker"—the reference to those eighteen million votes she garnered in the 2008 presidential race—got bumped. But at this point, maybe that resume item goes without saying.

As for those in the middle—those who love to hate and hate to love—a strong ambivalence exists. Many Democratic women demand that Hillary be perfect before they can offer their full support of a second White House run. They know they should back her since she supports issues like paid family leave and equal pay, but they cringe because of her vote supporting the Iraq War, her discussions about the plight of poor women from her über-privileged vantage point, or that ultimately she *did* "stand by her man," finding it impossible to forgive her for not leaving Bill. Since she was loyal, she is viewed by these doubtful women as someone who stayed in a marriage merely to advance her own political ambitions, something that feels inauthentic to them to such a degree that they don't trust her as a potential president, even though male candidates are rarely judged that way.

So as we zoom into the 2016 presidential election, it should be no surprise that the media and voters once again are off to the races with the familiar "love Hillary, love Hillary not" game. The question of why we engage in that love-hate game is a legitimate one to explore about the person who could well become the first woman president of the United States.

Why do we play the Hillary love-hate card with such vigor? I believe it's less about whether she voted for war in Iraq, what she knew about Benghazi, her votes in the Senate or, as she once infamously remarked, whether she should have forsaken her professional goals to stay home, bake cookies, and have teas. I think it's because she has dared to embrace, through her life, more than one version of herself, presenting a three-dimensional view of modern womanhood, rather than the pre-packaged 2-D portrayals so many of us expect of any politician, especially women, in the harsh national spotlight.

Hillary Clinton brazenly dared to step out, in the most public of ways, from our expectations of women in general and first ladies in particular. She landed in one of the most gendered roles in America, that of a First Lady of Arkansas, when her husband served as the youngest governor in the country, and she's been trying to escape the constraints of that role ever since. In 1992, at the age of 45, she was the kind of First Lady we had never seen on the national stage, someone who already was an accomplished professional in her own right with a life separate from that of her husband that she dared to cultivate. But for many voters, even decades after "women's lib," she was viewed more as a wife who didn't know her place rather than someone representing the majority of women at the time—those working outside the home in their own careers.

She was deemed too big for her britches. She was too ambitious for a politician's wife. She was too educated. She was too smart—some said smarter than her husband. Who knew whether we could trust a woman with that kind of agenda? That prevailing attitude became clear when Hillary used her education to work on federal health care reform during her husband's first term in the White House. Even when that determined effort failed, and she strategically changed her approach to a more traditional one, focusing on children and donning pink suits reminiscent of Jackie Kennedy, she was still considered suspect.

But why should we have been shocked that she had her own personal goals beyond practicing law and being married to Bill? As someone who was a product of a "revolution," who came of age on the cusp of a new wave of feminism, no one should have been surprised by her refusal to live by rules that governed our mothers and grandmothers. Because she was one of the first women in the public spotlight to embrace the ideas of the women's movement by being a full-time working mother, successful in her own right and, for a time, under her own name, women found things to dislike about her. They, in essence, turned on the very thing they longed to see in the public arena.

So it's not surprising that Hillary still gives us pause for other reasons, none of which seemingly have anything to do with her readiness or ours, to finally elect a woman president.

While Hillary doesn't poll well among men when being compared to male candidates, her biggest obstacle to becoming the first woman president of the United States is likely to be women voters themselves. Women often look at other women through an unbreakable gender lens they use to view and judge each other, despite feminism's best efforts. In today's "Oprah-fied" world, there seems to be an unspoken demand that women—including Hillary—be perfect. She must be perfectly authentic at every moment of every day, even though we know from our own pop culture soul-searching that such a thing is impossible. Perfect in pitch, perfect in dress, however each person defines womanly perfection. For some women, if there is any hint of contradiction or moment of inauthenticity in a 2016 campaign, Hillary will be toast and will find herself bidding goodbye to what is most likely her last chance at the White House.

Plenty of challenges exist in her 2016 quest. Can she count on the Millennials who helped Obama win? Some pundits predict that her daughter Chelsea, who straddles the Gen X and Millennial generations, will be key to convincing them. What about the certain sector of women who, believing that in 2008 we had become a post-feminist nation, felt a man would better advance their favored agenda? Many tween and teen girls in 2008 loved Hillary and were deeply invested in her campaign. They turned out in droves, along with their mothers, to support her so that their daughters, they hoped, could be part of electing America's first woman president. Have eight years dampened their youthful devotion? And where will the baby boomers land? After all, it was the baby boomers who helped to put Bill Clinton in the White House in 1992 and for a second term in 1996. Do they have Clinton fatigue as they enjoy retirement? Many from that generation say they admire Hillary but admit that they don't know whether they can vote for her again.

What we have is a Hillary paradox.

But how do we figure it all out? We know that media dissect her and scholars study her, but what do women—who are the key to winning national elections—think of her today? Are women still yearning for Hillary to break that infamous glass ceiling, or have they moved on?

The essays in *Love Her, Love Her Not: The Hillary Paradox* are intended to jumpstart a new conversation about Hillary Clinton as she makes her second run for the White House. This conversation should reflect honestly on whether we can examine the myriad reasons for loving or hating Hillary in order to move past our own personal issues with a qualified, complicated woman who wants to lead our country. We cannot have this conversation without asking whether that infamous "likability" factor will cost her votes, as it possibly did in 2008. Lastly, we must look deeply into our collective obsessions with Hillary and ask where they originate and what impact they could possibly have on Hillary's 2016 run.

There are so many lenses through which to view Hillary in a way we don't with men, and so much of it is based on her gender. Is Hillary the New Black? Is Bitch the new presidential? Is Grandma the new power player? How do the symbols of women's clothing impact our view of her? Has she made women feel braver because of her own choices? Will the relationships she built as First Lady of the United States and secretary of state actually matter if she is president? Can she build a campaign on her favored secretary of state issues of women and children? Will she escape the age issue and benefit from the power of the crone? How many repurposed sexist barbs will she have to endure? Should she just abandon the idea of the White House altogether and become a diplomat of the world? *Love Her, Love Her Not: The Hillary Paradox* explores our complicated relationship with Hillary Clinton through 28 provocative, humorous, and insightful essays written by women across the spectrums of age, political affiliation, and cultural backgrounds. Timely and fresh, these innovative perspectives will no doubt provoke much sought-after conversation we long for about Hillary, while the political and cultural dialogue about her rises to new levels. And, I hope, it will give all those who love to hate and hate to love new talking points about the woman who wants to shatter the highest political glass ceiling in this country. Ultimately, this collection of essays could help us decide whether we can finally elect a woman president and whether that woman is Hillary Clinton.

Joanne Cronrath Bamberger
November 2015

Worshipping the Semiotic Brilliance of Hillary's Pantsuits

Deb Rox

Hillary Clinton is my fashion icon. She is my Chanel, my New York Fashion Week, my WWD, my Anna Wintour, my Dolly Parton in a coat of many colors. I love her pantsuits. I love all of them, especially the black Oscar de la Renta ones with their sharp jacket lines. But more importantly than the pantsuits themselves, I love what they mean. Hillary has divined Buddha-level truths that are revealed in how she dresses, and I want everyone to worship at the altar of her glorious pantsuit world order.

I know the entire world does not join me in this view, and while I wish everyone would appreciate the gorgeousness of the matching two-piece, I'm absolutely certain Hillary doesn't care. That's the point, hard won and victorious, and I'm deeply inspired by it. We all could learn a few things from the powerful pantsuit.

Women my age have always needed Hillary, or at least I did. My mother's generation believed in the power of pearls and husbands, so I was more or less on my own to figure out what to wear and how to cope with obvious double standards and sexist rules.

I sauntered through the best sartorial year of my life when I was 12 years old, probably because it was my last shot at not being judged for dressing like a boy. I divined a uniform of sorts for daily wear: jeans and tees, except on Thursdays, when I wore my beloved Girl Scout uniform and power-badge-boasting sash. My only concern was maximizing wears of my favorite shirt, which sported a shiny, red-white-and-blue, groovy-fonted, ironed-on VOTE emblem in honor of the Bicentennial election—because the Bicentennial was cool and Jimmy Carter was my man. My tees were styling every day, but on VOTE days, my swagger was imbued with purpose and shine.

All of that changed the very next year when life became a complexity of hormones, gender performance, an acute awareness of class struggles, and new body insecurities that played out in the typical oppressive theater of a young woman's closet. Every morning was consumed by the question of what to wear, with option after option tried on, critiqued in a cruel fairytale mirror, and discarded into a pile that might as well have been fiery toxic garbage.

Boys seemed to trudge along through all of this in their same Levis, lucky bastards. They were blissfully free of the burden of daily decisions about how to present, adorn, or conceal their bodies. They had fewer distracting options, none of which seemed to limit what they did, whereas all of mine limited my activities, and all of mine seemed to define how feminine I was or wasn't, and how successful I was at understanding social and sexual politics.

Learning how to play an updated version of the pearl game, my friends were spending all of their cash on accessories, which accurately named how I was beginning to feel. I was a gender-bending young woman who wanted to accomplish things in a broken, sexist culture. Sidelined, expected to become the helper, the cheerleader but not the player, the accessory.

I delayed dealing with all of that as best as I could. I adopted a new wardrobe inspired by my beloved president: denim shirts and Oxford button downs, rolled up to the elbows. I was ready to get to work.

I've always felt most inspired by, most comforted by, the image of our leaders as workers. I live for the mythos of rolling up sleeves and getting things done. Give me a stump speech in a parking lot over a State of the Union any day. I need that part of the American Dream, the dreamy part, the part where we set sights high and then grab a pickaxe or a pen and begin to build. Our leaders express that in their rolled-up sleeves, and they show that in their power suits, too. Suits, with their tailored pockets and their boxy shoulders and sturdy fabric, might not be coal-mine attire, but they connote work that is powerful in other ways. Suits are modern armor, and in their monochromatic simplicity and uniformity, they remind wearers that they are all steely arms of the same machine. When you are wearing a suit, first you walk across a tarmac or a hallway in Congress to sign things, the ink of your pen matching the dark threads of your jacket, and then you remove that jacket, roll up your sleeves, and get to it.

But that "you" used to always be a man. A woman in a suit was a poseur: it was called "menswear chic" so that we always remembered we were borrowing "his" power. Sometimes I love the power that choice carried for women, but I didn't always love how wearing it could backfire and be something of a dog whistle for backlash attacks. The politics of menswear is fraught with the connotations of male aggression, sexual identity and expression included. Sometimes that's awesome; sometimes that's not the point.

Similarly, the "collar" in blue- and white-collar work is a man's collar. The boys of my generation who wanted positions of power moved easily from jeans to uniforms or suits. Boys move easily into power and into being seen as leaders. If girls and women want that, they have to endure cultural fashion madness to get it. They have to run through the streets of Pamplona dodging glitter and lace and apron strings and empire waists and corsets and demi-cupped foundational garments and hat hair and bejeweled necklines and mesh cover-ups and pantyhose hatched from eggs and ruffles and spandex, constantly changing everything. They have to find a style that says just what they want it to say, factoring in trends, appropriateness to the setting, gender identity, signaling their relative pear-shapedness, the male-defined and limiting scale of frigid-to-slutty heel height, and more.

Men have to have their inseam and neck measured.

Women have to come out red-carpet ready on the other side of the gauntlet, dressed for success when success means working twice as hard under ten times the scrutiny.

Hillary has managed to do that, and I have learned from her. That is why I would love to see inside Hillary's closet. I would love to run my hand across the sleeves of her jackets, lined up like guards. She's learned lessons the hard way on the road to a wardrobe of tailored basics, and I want to absorb all of her knowledge. I want to master the semiotics of Hillary's pantsuits.

So my years of coming into my own agency as a worker, my post-Carter years, were like many of my generation. We added plaid to our denim and became activists against all that Ronald Reagan brought to our fair land. For me that meant feminist activism, which eventually led to employment as an educator and non-profit worker. The move from activist to professional who needed to be taken seriously in state buildings and with funders wasn't easy. Again, I envied my male colleagues with their easy uniforms, their power ties and shirts bought in bulk. Did I really have to wear pantyhose and pumps? My clothes, all of our clothes and where they landed on a gendered scale, seemed to signify so much to others, yet I had no idea how to strike the right balance. Did I have to wear pearls? Others went that route. Hillary did. Did wearing the wrong accessory for a woman peg me as someone only cut out to be an accessory?

It's not just clothes, of course. Politics are a cruel beauty crucible for women. The more attention a woman has for her appearance, the less qualified she appears. But not tending to fashion and style connotes breaking all sorts of norms. Worse, when a woman is attached to a policy agenda, her appearance, and her very body, are up for vote brokering.

There is no way for a woman to win against the double standards of female body judgment. Nancy Pelosi is horribly slammed because her face is thin and shows signs of aging (as though aging in an experienced leader is a bad thing), but Michelle Obama's "guns" are disparaged as too mannish. If simple sexist scrutiny isn't enough, Photoshop is deployed to turn appearance into jokes. When the video of Sarah Palin's swimsuit competition in the 1980s was released, hot mama memes exploded to solidify the trivializing MILF jokes posed against her. Michele Bachmann's eyes are shown as crazed. Inherent in the "F" in MILF is the pernicious reminder that women are continually judged on whether men find them sexually appealing.

To thick or too thin. Too feminine, too not. Too sexy, too not. Clothing choices on top of this are suspect because they are skewered as representative of a woman leader's character. It's the embodiment of her morning choice, after all. Can you vote for a woman who chooses a floral blouse, a mannish flannel jacket, a grosgrain ribbon headband, THOSE shoes? We so rarely ask those questions of men because we don't see men's clothing; we see that steely machine. Women, quite literally, can't win.

No one has been assaulted by this wrecked rhetoric more than Hillary Clinton. The media's obsession with judging her clothing, hair, height, weight, facial expressions—even the shape of her highly functional ankles—has been a leading domestic gross national product for years.

Despite all that, Hillary won. She won office, yes, but she also "won" this look-ist scrutiny that trickles down and ruins women everywhere. Hillary, quite literally, found a way to win that second battle with pantsuits.

What Hillary did with pantsuits was nothing short of genius.

She had worn suits and jackets among other fashion choices in those early years, but as her leadership was tempered by opposition, she took the enemy's arrows and wove them into a standard uniform of a simple tailored jacket and matching slacks. You want to focus on her ankles? Here's a pantsuit. You want to call her pejoratives like "dyke" for claiming power? Here's another pantsuit. You want to assume things about her as a parent or wife? Here's another pantsuit.

Those brilliant pantsuits were the new Girl Scout uniform meets futuristic unitard meets Wonder Woman bracelets. They deflected. They defined. They won.

Hillary didn't invent the pantsuit or its usefulness to working women, but from her massive platform, women like me watched her distill gendered expectations and the entire sartorial vocabulary of powerful men into one distinct image that said everything that needed to be said. By the time she moved on from her role as First Lady, she wore it on the campaign trail, in her Senate office, on the streets of New York City following 9/11, on tarmacs before and after flying over 950,000 miles as our most traveled secretary of state, in the most important hallways of the world, from daybreak until midnight. Hillary's pantsuits stared down Putin, pundits, and perpetual dirty pool. In response, Hillary's pantsuits said *power, efficiency, urgency; I'm ahead of you.* They said, *I'm here, and I'm here to work.*

We watched her evolve into this: from a First Lady in pearls who reinvented the position of presidential spouse to a powerful leader in her own right. In pantsuits.

This mastery against all odds is something I admire and I want to replicate. It's a gift to women like me who will never reach Hillary heights in leadership but who nonetheless want unfettered agency in a still-sexist world, and who want to change those conditions.

It's also a stunning example of disarming an enemy. The way Hillary guided this conversation was an object lesson in control. Knowing she'd never be free from attacks and scrutiny that would play out through her appearance, she targeted the sights onto one question. Instead of a litany of hair/cankles/skirt length questions, or assessment of where she fell on the "appropriately feminine" clothing scale, she forced the debate to the singularity of "what color pantsuit is she wearing today?" In doing so, Hillary degendered the playing field, making her appearance effectively recede to a question almost as innocuous as "what color is his tie today?"

She let them have something: the pantsuit. She gave them one thing to objectify, and in doing so, she controlled the conversation. Hillary owned the pantsuit singularly, and then when she veered from it, glamorously and casually—and yes, with pearls, because pearls are beautiful when they are your choice—even that was in her control, on her terms. When you are known for your pantsuits, you can easily disarm by simply wearing a tunic.

Most of us don't have this Art of War, Diplomacy, and Pantsuits figured out, and we can learn so much from it. You know, Hillary titled her 2014 memoir *Hard Choices* to speak a common truth about the human experience, about political life, and about the way we all shape and interpret character. We make so many choices, with the first one every day being what to wear, and it's still infinitely more fraught for women than it is for men.

I'm choosing the pantsuit, at least what the Clinton pantsuit means about narrowing distractions and taking control of obstacles, in order to claim power. In order to roll up my sleeves and get to work. Ease with these things may have been given to men as their birthright, but at least I'm lucky that leaders like Hillary, with her closet of many colored pantsuits, have figured out workable solutions for me.

I Don't Need Hillary Clinton to Be Perfect

Joanne Cronrath Bamberger

I confess that in 2008 I didn't think we were a country that was ready for a woman president. Oh, how I wanted us to be! The geeky political science major in me wanted voters to see that it was finally time for a woman to move into the White House in her own right, and not as a First Lady. The 1970s feminist in me—the one who was schooled about über-conservative Phyllis Schlafly's political efforts to keep women in the home, the possibility of an Equal Rights Amendment, and the "women's lib" expectations that I would, of course, see a woman president in my lifetime—assumed that in the twenty-first century things finally were changing. Yes, we were still waiting for our very own Margaret Thatcher or Indira Gandhi. Yes, many countries had already zoomed past us on that milestone like Ireland, the Philippines, Sri Lanka, Liberia, Kosovo, Switzerland, and more. In 2008, how could it not be time for the United States finally to join that club?

By the time Senator Hillary Clinton announced her bid for the White House, I was much older than I thought I'd be when we would finally see a "viable" woman presidential candidate. I'd become a middle-aged mom with a couple of good careers under my belt, but I was much further down the road of life than I'd dreamed I'd be when a woman had a serious shot at finally sitting in the Oval Office as commander in chief, rather than as an adviser or VP or FLOTUS. To be honest, it didn't hurt my excitement about Hillary that, in some ways, she was like me: a woman of a certain generation (although we are at opposite ends of the baby boomer crowd!) who wanted to make a difference, a mother of a daughter, a woman with a law degree who wasn't afraid to speak up, and someone who felt like politics was in her blood. Of course, that connection wasn't hurt by the fact that we both owned a pair of those vintage striped jeans she was wearing in the now famous *LIFE* magazine photo spread from her Wellesley College days.

As we watched her jump into the race, my then-third-grade daughter and I were both more than "ready" for Hillary.

While polls showed that America was statistically on board with the idea of a woman president eight years ago, the worry in my gut knew that women like Hillary—and, yes, like me—often weren't taken seriously in the world of old (and new) boys' networks and that there were still too many gendered ideas about how women *should* be that held us all back, Hillary included, from what we *could* be. Sadly, my gut correctly predicted that the 2008 election cycle wasn't going to be the Year of the Woman President in America; it took me longer to figure out why.

Hillary fell short because she wasn't perfect.

Hillary Clinton has had a perfection problem for years. She wasn't our idea of a perfect First Lady because she dared to step out of the mold of what voters knew and were comfortable with. She wasn't the picture of perfection as a Senate candidate because what FLOTUS had ever dared to tout her own qualifications to run for national office? She wasn't the perfect wife because she stayed with her straying husband, and she wasn't the perfect wife because many assumed she stayed for reasons of ambition rather than marital loyalty; that didn't sit well with women regardless of whether they were baby boomers, Gen Xers or Millennials. She wasn't perfect because she turned all our expectations on their heads about women politicians. In 2008, she was still a transitional woman trying to navigate the gap between twentieth century stay-at-home First Ladies and the first generation of accomplished feminist women who were going to "have it all," whether voters were ready for that or not.

But why did we project those expectations and visions of American womanhood onto Hillary? Why do so many of us still, years later, want her to be perfect, however we define that, when we don't expect it of any man who's run for the White House, or even any other political office? We've all pretty much accepted the fact that her husband is less than perfect and that the woman in the blue dress who almost got him kicked out of office certainly wasn't. Yet, we've absolved both Bill, as he's become the major global statesman, and Monica Lewinsky, as many laud her anti-bullying TED talk comeback. But when it comes to Hillary, many voters still hold it against her for tenaciously clinging to her own dreams and making personal compromises many of us contend we would never have made in order to achieve them.

Maybe Hillary's loss to Barack Obama is better framed this way. Even in 2008, our society still expected women to be like Mary Poppins, practically perfect in every way; without that, our country wasn't ready to give Hillary, or any other woman, the keys to the White House.

We clearly still live in a time where women are criticized and judged more harshly than men based on this expectation of perfection. That obvious, but unspoken, need for female perfection plays out in so many parts of our lives. It's what fuels the "mommy wars," our debates about "leaning in" vs. institutional changes for increases in women's professional advancement, and the sales of women's magazines, books, and websites that call on us to continually examine the things that are wrong—or imperfect—with our lives. But it's not just men who expect us to continually tweak our lives to achieve some level of model womanhood. Too many women expect perfection of themselves, as well, and end up projecting that onto candidate Hillary. If we, as twenty-first century American women, judge ourselves harshly for failing at the perfection game, how can we not view Hillary through that same lens?

There are plenty of people who say that Hillary fell short of her White House dreams because of her own Clinton "baggage" dating as far back as her years as First Lady of Arkansas. But if we open that matched set, as well as our own, and take a closer look, we don't have to search very far for proof of the perfection theory. Articles abound examining our perfection culture, including one notable 2012 *Newsweek* piece entitled "Why Women Should Stop Trying to Be Perfect," written not by a pop culture guru, but by Debora Spar, the president of Barnard College, who described many mid-life women "… as a generation desperate to be perfect wives, mothers, and professionals."

Obviously, about eighteen million Americans thought Hillary was perfect enough, even with the relentless gendered media references wondering whether she was "relatable" or "authentic," not-so-subtle suggestions that a woman president needed to be more than just qualified; but in order to win at that moment in time she had to reflect an image of traditional American womanhood.

The truth behind that fear of a less-than-perfect woman daring to be the most powerful person in the world was summed up in one unforgettable moment in the January 2008 Democratic debate in New Hampshire when one of the moderators asked Hillary what she would say to voters who favored her political track record but who thought Barack Obama was a more "likable" person.

"Well … that hurts my feelings…. But I'll try to go on," she quipped, trying to make light of an obviously ridiculous question for a presidential candidate. If "likable" was a presidential qualification, I'm pretty sure neither Richard Nixon nor Lyndon Johnson, among others, would ever have been elected.

Hillary's response was received by laughs and applause in the live audience. Her reaction was stereotypically feminine; she deflected in jest and embraced the laughs that came at her own expense. Few would probably even remember that moment today, but for an unnecessarily opportunistic jab from her main competition.

Looking somewhat smug, candidate Barack Obama, barely giving her a side-eye glance, made the now-infamously cutting, yet telling, remark that made so many women cringe: "You're likable enough, Hillary."

That four-word smack-down from the likable guy—who wasn't being so likable in that moment—was the very definition of the double standard still being applied to women who dared to seek out political power. You'd better be perfectly likable and authentic (however each voter defines that authenticity) or suffer the electoral consequences. And if you're an ambitious woman whose attempts at being powerful and likable don't translate as authentic? Well, heaven help you.

But that's the nut. Somehow, in less than one minute on the national stage, only being "likable enough" for Hillary Clinton became synonymous with not perfect enough, reinforcing the social dynamic about powerful women and how they are treated by powerful men. Sadly, the odds are that this same idea will create problems for her again in her second White House run. As research by the Barbara Lee Family Foundation has found, "while male politicians can attract voters' support by appearing strong and decisive, even when they are not perceived as being particularly likable, women still have to prove to the world they are both qualified for office and likable."

Fast-forward a few years from that infamous debate moment to an interview with *Glamour* magazine in which Hillary advised young women that, "You don't have to be perfect. Most men never think like that." While the second sentence is true, I wish the first one were, too. But the truth is that we live in a world where women are expected to be perfect, most especially the person who wants to be the first woman president of the United States.

But I don't need the first woman president to be perfect; I'm pretty sure I'm not alone. And I don't need her to be any more or less likable than any other person who thinks he or she is qualified for the job. As a woman who's lived through the shared era of "women's lib," I've learned the hard way that liberation came with an unspoken bargain—you can break out of the mold of your mother and grandmother, but to succeed, you will have to be perfect in the eyes of men. Perfect on the job. Perfect with the kids. Perfect in not complaining about the unreasonable demands that come with expecting women who try to "have it all" to be perfect while doing it. Some people say those days are over. But one only has to look around to see that today that demand for female perfection just comes with other labels, like reinvention, redefining success, and looking for a third metric.

So the big question for us in 2016 is whether we can move beyond our collective need for Hillary to be pitch perfect, whatever that means to each one of us. And is that possible when we live in a time when women now are being sold an additional narrative: if you're not perfect, don't worry, there's still time to achieve it regardless of your age. Perfection can come as a third phase of life with new purpose and meaning. It's okay as you enter your 50s or 60s to step back, slow down, take a nap, and look for a "third metric" where female success is redefined, according to Arianna Huffington, "beyond money and power."

Now, the idea of taking things a little slower is as appealing to me as the next gal, but is that code for giving up on long-held personal ambitions that possibly have something to do with political power or leadership? Or is that just a nicer way of saying it's time to bow out, to channel our grandmotherly feelings and count the days until we hop on our ice floes? It's almost as if a woman of a certain age who isn't toying with prioritizing getting more sleep and stepping off the professional ladder is somehow not perfect enough for her time and generation. It makes me wonder, is perfection being redefined to cut the legs out from under experienced, powerful women leaders? And, if so, how will that impact a second Hillary Clinton run for the White House?

As a woman invested in politics and the future of this country, I don't need Hillary to be perfect or to reinvent herself or to strive for some touchy, feely third metric. I don't need her to be the perfect *Commander in Chief*, as was portrayed on TV by Geena Davis, or even to have been the perfect secretary of state like Téa Leoni in *Madam Secretary*. I'm guessing many other women feel the same way. And, to be honest, I don't want her to be perfect. Because if she has to be without flaws, that's much too high of a bar for any woman who comes after her. And it's too high of a bar for the rest of us.

What I need from Hillary is for her to be a leader who will listen to her constituents.

What I need from Hillary is for her to show my daughter that it is more than acceptable to be an ambitious woman with your own dreams and aspirations of leadership without being perceived as calculating and power hungry. What I need from Hillary is for her to break not only the highest glass ceiling; I need her to break the perfection myth, as well.

Imperfection is what we've gotten in all our previous presidents. We've learned the hard way that Barack Obama wasn't really as authentically likable as many people thought he was in 2008. We learned that the smiling politician who gives a rousing "let's all come together speech" also has his own sharp edges and sharp tongue that often make him not so likable. Maybe it's time to admit that likability and perceived perfection aren't the best checklist items on which to judge a candidate.

The only perfection I need is to see a woman who shares my political beliefs sitting behind that desk in the Oval Office in my lifetime. If that day comes, that will be the most perfect of all days for me, especially if I get to see it with my daughter.

On Being Hillary's Campaign BFF
Amy Ferris

Dear Hillary,

I want you to think of me as a kinda, sorta *BFF*. Or, better yet, a very best friend forever: a *VBFF*. You know, someone you can share your secrets with. Okay, well, maybe not secrets, maybe that's stretching it. How about, you know, a friend who you can call at any hour, ungodly or not? I mean, really, why is 3 a.m. ungodly? Why not 7 a.m.? Or 5 a.m.? 5 a.m. seems wholly ungodly to me. But, as always, I digress.

I wanna be a woman—*the woman*—you can share your deepest, darkest, most consuming worries with (notice I didn't say secrets). Someone you can chat with about, you know, anything. Anything. Everything. Everything from your money worries (okay, not a popular topic when you're making 300 grand to speak) to your hair stylist (love the hair, a keeper) to your wardrobe consultant (maybe a simple A-line skirt now and then) to your astrologer (a Scorpio, just like my dad) and such. *And such* being a whole lot of stuff, right? I mean there is so much to talk about and share. *And such* can be anything from why wear flats to maybe even a marital crisis or problem, and not necessarily yours, someone else's.

I just wanna give you some sage advice—a little bit of wisdom—as you're running again for the White House in 2016.

Girl to Girl.

Woman to Woman.

Warrior to Warrior.

Goddess to Goddess.

WOmentor to WOmenter.

Women really, truly, deeply want the truth.

Really.

Seriously.

Truly.

I know we always say we want the truth, but then when we hear it—when we hear the truth—sometimes, not always, but sometimes, we kinda cringe, cover our ears, and start singing or humming loudly, making believe we didn't hear it. Because the truth stings. Hurts. Does it ever. But we do wanna hear it. Trust me on that. And many women—many, many women—knew the minute you said you weren't going to be a stay-at-home mom, baking cookies, that you were *(and are)* a ball of fierce. You are fierce and mighty, and dare I say, *one tough cookie.* One tough broad. Back in '92, even before Bill became president, even before he was elected, you said during a *60 Minutes* interview—and yes, I am quoting—*"I'm not sitting here—some little woman standing by her man like Tammy Wynette. I'm sitting here because I love him and respect him ..."* But you did stand by your man. Yes, you did. For years and years. Even with—especially with—all the hoopla around Monica, and everything surrounding that, you did stand by him. You stood by Bill through thick and, yes, thin (and one or two were very thin, unattractively thin), and I am sure there are some women—okay, many, like hundreds of thousands, maybe even millions—who wanna know why. I mean, that's a huge, hot button topic—sexual infidelity—and I think it's one big-ass issue that is always gonna sneak in, and sneak up, and quite honestly, I hate to say it, bite you in the ass as you run, and you need to have a good answer. A really good answer, not a shrug, not a, "that's my business and no one else's" (even though, truthfully, yes, it really is only your business and no one else's). You're gonna have to own this one. I know, right? Big fucking deal, what's past is past. I get it. Why air dirty laundry? Everyone has a past. I know I do. But having a past, and having it thrown up in your face repeatedly, well, hell, that's a whole different ball of candle wax.

And sure, sure, folks are gonna come after you, badger you, attack you about huge, gigantic, massive world issues. You know, like ISIS, Iraq, Jordan, the Middle East, Benghazi, terrorism, global warming (and a huge host of environmental issues), Ebola, foreign aid, world hunger, religious fanaticism, Syria, fair trade, nuclear war and weapons, along with a host of issues right in your own—our own—backyard, so to speak. There's the complete disappearance of the middle-class, gun violence, homelessness, poverty, veteran's issues, mental health issues, racism, sexism, domestic violence, violence against women, human trafficking, children's rights, human rights, the drug problem, legalization of marijuana, gay rights, women's rights, health care, Obamacare, censorship, and of course, your secretary of state years.

But here's the thing, as your newly appointed VBFF, which is sorta like a campaign manager without all the sexy benefits, let me just say this, toss this out: women look up to you; women wanna be you and have that amazing, powerful, almighty Hillary effect, not to mention that glorious, contagious laugh. And just like you—fierce, amazing, awesome you—they wanna be the kind of women hurricanes are named after, so, maybe you oughta think about this just a bit as you run.

If you wanna hold onto the blue states, you're gonna have to talk about the blue dress. My guess, my honest to goodness guess, is that you won't be judged for speaking the truth, you'll grab a couple of red states, and you'll be elected.

Best and warm,
Amy

How Can Hillary Be Herself When She's a Stand-In?

Mary C. Curtis

It's a familiar knock on Hillary Clinton, one that's deadly for any politician hoping to occupy the White House—she has a hard time being herself.

Yes, that authenticity thing.

It's true that sometimes for Clinton the warmth that friends swear is obvious in small groups and one-on-one conversations fails to break through in auditoriums or on a formal debate stage. That's something I observed when the 2008 campaign trail swung through South Carolina, and the warm smile and funny spontaneity that lit up some smaller gatherings did not always translate.

But is that really all her fault? So many people expect so much of Clinton because she had the fortune or misfortune of being born in October 1947, a prototypical baby boomer, touched by ever-shifting attitudes and changes—legal and otherwise—on issues that redefined America.

From race to class to gender to relationships to motherhood to grandmotherhood and more, Hillary Clinton has been there: experiencing, achieving, and experimenting. And so were so many others who now expect a lot from her. To take one trivial example, who doesn't change hairstyles? But when Clinton shifts from curly to straight, from long to short or—goodness gracious—adds a headband, it's dissected for weighty political and psychological significance.

Is it that the woman, lawyer, wife, mother, First Lady, and maybe one day president of the United States has trouble being herself, or that so many are seeing themselves and their own life choices in a changing America, looking to her when they could be looking within? She caught the wave and the backlash, the support and defensiveness, the good and the bad, and like many on the edge of change, she has sometimes been judged more as a symbol than as a human being. It's pretty hard to just be you when you're a poster girl, and folks are looking at every move under a microscope. For some you're a representative and an icon, and for others, a dislikable caricature.

Hillary Clinton has always stood out, from the time she was the hard-working, overachieving young student in the Chicago suburbs to her perch as the prohibitive favorite to be the Democratic presidential nominee in 2016.

One wonders if a film to re-introduce her—one similar to her husband's 1992 convention show-stopper, the biographical *Man from Hope*—is in the works. In her case, would a movie be seen as more reinvention, since Clinton has been in the public eye for so many years? Though she certainly has her own story to tell, so much of her identity has been forged in relation to others and to society, like so many other women.

Take that husband, Bill Clinton, both a blessing and a curse. Her public introduction to most Americans was a *60 Minutes* appearance cleaning up after reports of his infidelity threatened to derail his 1992 presidential campaign. Even then, it was all about him. Her remarks, though, on standing by her man, rankled those who were fans of legendary country and western singer Tammy Wynette or saw hypocrisy since Hillary *was* there to stand by Bill. A later swipe at those who stayed home to bake cookies was an unnecessary self-inflicted wound.

She became "Hillary Clinton," stalwart wife and not exactly

happy to be in that position—one that put her smack in the middle of debates about gender roles, relationship expectations, and the working woman vs. stay-at-home wife/mother "wars."

She was a First Lady full of talent and ambition, a transitional figure carrying 1960s cultural baggage. It took time for many Americans to get used to her powerful presence—one that still makes some uncomfortable and a bit resentful, as she derived some of that power and much of her visibility from marriage even though she had accomplished much before she ever met her husband—a story so many women share. Whether you thought she was an independent woman deliberately holding back or someone along for the ride depended on your generation and/or point of view.

No wonder it was hard to see the person underneath.

As for the husband, the bad and good Bill Clinton was and will always be linked to the fortunes of Hillary Clinton. Despite all her many pre- and post-Bill achievements and honors—the first student commencement speaker at Wellesley College, the first female partner at the prestigious Rose Law Firm—she decided to use Clinton as her last name instead of Rodham to make the couple more palatable to more traditional Arkansas voters around the time Bill Clinton hoped to retake the governor's office in 1982. In her successful campaign to be a U.S. senator from New York, she visited every county in the state, but no doubt her role as First Lady boosted her efforts.

Their relationship has always been in the public eye the way few have. You know the saying that no one knows the truth about any relationship other than one's own? Not so when it comes to the Clintons and their host of bold critics, with many convinced it is more political calculation than marriage. Why else would she get the mix of admiration and scorn when she decided to stay in their marriage after her husband's infidelities? Her poll ratings reached a high during Bill Clinton's "Monica" troubles. But she was probably the last person who wanted to be seen as a victim.

In that 2008 primary in South Carolina, although Hillary's name was on the ballot, it was Bill Clinton who started to suck all the oxygen out of the room and step on more than a few toes. The sentiment of her fans at one of his appearances on her behalf: "I like her, but if she's elected, who, really, is going to be calling the shots?"

If navigating the changing terrain of gender roles in work and relationships was one defining issue of Hillary Clinton's coming of age, America's coming to terms with its complicated history on race was certainly another. Clinton found herself at the intersection of race and gender in her 2008 campaign, with unwanted help from her husband.

Bill Clinton made remarks that some voters I spoke with then, particularly African Americans, thought disrespected the legitimacy of her rival Barack Obama. Hillary Clinton was tagged as racially insensitive when she said before that primary that "the power" of Martin Luther King's dream became "real in people's lives" because of a president, Lyndon B. Johnson, who "got it accomplished." It all became part of the story, and her campaign seemed to crumble at that moment.

That insinuation must have hurt Hillary Clinton, who, after Yale Law School, had gone to work for Marian Wright Edelman, founder of the Children's Defense Fund. Clinton's resume is filled with work on behalf of children and social justice issues. Edelman became a mentor, although their relationship frayed in the 1990s because of disagreements over the effectiveness and safety net provisions in President Bill Clinton's welfare reform legislation. But they have since made peace. In 2010, when the Marian Wright Edelman Public Library of Marlboro County opened in Edelman's Bennettsville, South Carolina, hometown— where such public facilities were once segregated by race—the Clintons sent a letter to mark the celebration of the place and a $100,000 donation from the William J. Clinton Foundation.

In 2008, the charismatic politician who came out on top was

Obama, an African-American candidate whose star burned a bit brighter than Hillary Clinton's. His anti–Iraq War stance and pioneering achievements were rehashes of 1960s clashes that Clinton still found herself in the middle of, like it or not. Some of her supporters, who saw progress for women and African Americans as zero sum—a pick-sides choice that entangled even the ever-popular Obama-supporter Oprah Winfrey in controversy—tainted Clinton when the nastiness and bitterness that's a part of any political campaign took racism vs. sexism significance. Again, Hillary Clinton was caught in symbolic history. When, in defeat, she embraced her feminist icon status more than she had in early primaries, others speculated whether she had done too little too late.

But in Charlotte, North Carolina, in 2014 as Clinton was campaigning for Kay Hagan's U.S. Senate reelection bid—unsuccessfully, it turned out—she seemed comfortable tapping into what might be the next frontier. She name-checked her granddaughter, Charlotte, and segued into discussions of family, equality, and opportunity. "The American dream should be there for every single child," she seemed comfortable saying.

In a country where grandfathers in a presidential race are nothing new, Clinton would again be breaking ground, provoking expectations for a grandmother-in-chief. Ambivalent feelings toward relationships and work, love, and play cloud decisions everyone makes. In Hillary Clinton's case, she can't help being a very visible stand-in.

She embodies almost every human contradiction as she seeks to make her mark in politics, where we look for certainty, even when we know that our own authentic selves have those same contradictions.

She is Hillary Clinton, one woman, not everywoman. But with a legion of supporters and detractors who think they know all there is to know, proving that—being judged that way, even with an extensive record—will always be tougher than it seems.

A Crone of My Own: Hillary Clinton and the Gen X Feminist Experience

Faiqa Khan

Recently, there has been an uptick in literature and visual media that emphasizes the backstory of "crones." An archetypal figure that is as old as human storytelling, the crone is the mysterious female figure that sets heroes upon a path to success or exists as an obstacle to their quest. Whether through a wildly successful musical rebranding of Wicked Witches or television shows dissecting Snow White's wicked stepmother, we, as a society, have become concerned with understanding what makes a powerfully and, sometimes, fatally ambitious woman who she is.

The connection between a society's storytelling holds a direct link with that society's realities. Sometimes, those links are consciously constructed and, at other times, not. As America negotiates the meaning of the archetypal crone, it's worth considering our everyday reality as source for inspiration. Even the most cursory searches for our own crone will lead to one figure who has no equal: Hillary Clinton.

Hillary Clinton occupies various statuses in our society, but her influence is uncontested. Points of disagreement arise, however, when we are asked about the nature of that leadership. Is her role in our political landscape nefarious, virtuous, or both? Furthermore, is the same society that has traced the experiences of Sleeping Beauty's evil fairy queen also prepared to trace the origins of our own living archetype's rise to power?

For many, this examination of Hillary Clinton is a revisitation. As Millennials emerge as an important deciding factor in the next presidential elections, this retracing becomes necessary. It's a primer, not just aimed at gleaning information that can offer insight into political decisions about Hillary's potential bid for the presidency, but also into the story of how the fires of public perception have fashioned today's female leadership.

As young women my age set out to understand womanhood in the 1990s, we encountered our own specific struggles. The first and second waves of feminism had already occurred. The backlash of the eighties was fresh. With all this happening before us, young women of this time were embarking on a precarious third wave which had the added difficulties associated with culture, race, religion, and identity. I was a young woman coming of age in a politically and socially conservative state and a South Asian Muslim home. To say my journey toward a fully liberated understanding of womanhood was fraught with inconsistencies and obstacles would be an understatement. It was at this time in my life that Hillary Clinton emerged as my own crone.

For the female Generation Xers questing into womanhood, more was learned in the 1990s from Hillary Clinton by examining the manner in which she was *treated* rather than her direct advisement. She was largely viewed as ambitious and calculating. This perceived nature marked Hillary, and, whether conscious or not, I believe the women of my generation took note of the costs associated with such perception.

I was eighteen when I saw the now largely forgotten *60 Minutes* interview regarding Gennifer Flowers—Bill Clinton's alleged paramour—but it left a distinct impression upon me. My eyes were slowly opening to the realities of womanhood. This moment on *60 Minutes* was not much different than the less-salacious everyday moments when the women in my life often had to excuse or pardon their husbands' behavior in an effort to preserve the bigger picture. It was a squelching down of justified anger in favor of the greater good. Nonetheless, "standing by her man" was still perceived by many of her detractors as a sign of Hillary's fervent dedication to her own ambitions. These perceptions weren't the province of pundits alone. In a *Saturday Night Live* spoof of the reality show *Cops*, police officers arrive at a trailer where a distraught Bill Clinton plays a victimized spouse who refuses to press charges against his rough-talking, cigarette-smoking, abusive wife: Hillary. In this skit, it became painfully obvious how threatening a strong woman could be, even to the man who occupied one of the most powerful positions in the world. We laughed at this episode, but we also learned from our crone. We could be ambitious, but we must take care not to appear *too* ambitious.

Hillary emerged in the '90s as a central figure in most Clinton-era scandals. Details notwithstanding, I remember the crux of Whitewater rested upon Hillary's execution of her job as a lawyer and a perceived unethical grab at influence and wealth. The fact that *this* is the lasting impression for me only serves to underscore the idea that the neoconservative interpretations regarding the pitfalls of feminism were triumphantly vindicated through her persecution. The fires of public perception whispered into the ears of an emergent generation of new women: *Ambition in women equates with corruption, and, if you are unchecked, those ambitions will derail the virtuous efforts of men.*

Was Hillary's appearance at the epicenter of President Clinton's scandals the cause of a "vast right-wing conspiracy" as she herself maintained? Or was the First Lady actually a harbinger of chaos in her husband's political life? My suspicion is that it was neither. Realistically, our society and the media chose to consume her through a filter constructed in the aftershocks of the previous decade, which was aimed at discrediting feminism as a whole.

Neocon groups in the eighties and early nineties, many of them headed by women, stood before America and disparaged the spirit of equality that lay at the heart of the feminist movements of the '60s and '70s. We believed the made-up statistics of how "most women" preferred a "more traditional" family. This was bunk, of course, as Gallup polls in the early 1980s indicated exactly the opposite: that 60 percent of women were enthusiastic supporters of the Equal Rights Amendment and the impact it may have had upon women's lives.

Hillary Clinton then stood at the center of each scandal and was offered up to the American public for consumption. "You see? This is what happens when women seek to be 'equal' in their influence!!" The unspoken message here was that it was best for women to limit their influence over the men in their lives as well as society. To ignore the nefarious effects of Hillary was to choose walking upon a path of chaos and corruption.

There are lessons in life that do not sit easy, and yet they are grudgingly carried for want of a better lesson. I think this was apt in the case of my experience with Hillary Clinton as First Lady. I watched from afar as her husband's detractors used her to pick away at their shared work. For a while, she would disappear from the media's focus, only to reemerge every few years in the context of scandal or political flubbery. She lived in my mind throughout the nineties as a martyr to the cause of female ambition and influence. Time would show us later just how contrived this perception was. Hillary Clinton became a U.S. senator, she emerged as a viable presidential candidate, she went on to lead as the secretary of state, her marriage survived, her daughter thrived, and she even became a grandma. With every iteration of her public and personal success, our experience with her is more and more positive. She has transcended her role as the neocon's favorite anti-feminist symbol and evolved into a crone in the most positive sense of the word.

As my crone, Hillary's life has offered guidance to those of us on the quest toward female equality. Her appearances, though not as fleeting as before, are not quite prolific. We have learned to manage the bursts of wisdom from her and about her with a general sense of moderation. The question, though, is whether or not American women are prepared to transform our crone into a leader.

The crone is not a pervasive figure. She appears only when needed. A president is not a crone; it is a figure that occupies daily conversations. Are we ready for this iteration of Hillary?

Clinton's transformation from the figure that appears sporadically to offer wisdom into a grand architect who shapes the backdrop of our political reality is, in part, dependent on how much American women can stomach confronting our *own* capacity for power, leadership, and ambition. It is once again fashionable to state that women should operate in a reality with few limitations. Hillary shows us, however, that society often insists on stoking the flames of limitation that tell us ambition in women exists as a contradiction to the public's good. Her future role in American politics and our own will be largely resolved by our determination to see her and ourselves transcend these limitations.

Hillary Clinton Changed My Life
Jennifer Hall Lee

Hillary Clinton and her myriad personal and political experiences have made me a braver person than I used to be. Looking back on the 2008 primary campaign for the Democratic presidential nomination, I can connect the events that ultimately changed how I see myself as a political person.

As a volunteer on Hillary's campaign, for eight months, I made numerous phone calls to super-delegates and members of the National Organization for Women. Until then, I'd never followed Hillary's life or career too closely. I only became a volunteer after I saw the sexism that was thrown her way by fellow Democrats as she campaigned; that sexism prompted me to learn more about her as a person and as a candidate. I didn't realize at the time how strongly sexism would ultimately shape Hillary's campaign and its outcome, as well as my view of the political world.

At the time, I was working on a documentary film about the women's liberation movement and had a full-time job in the film industry as a visual effects editor. My daughter was five years old; the time demands of motherhood were still new for me. Nevertheless, I managed to schedule my campaign volunteer work during lunch breaks and in the few hours I had after I got home. It was the first time I ever volunteered for a presidential political campaign. Was it hard? Yes. But it was transformational.

It was explained to me once in the early days of my visual effects work on feature films that although the work seemed difficult and abstract, one day I would understand its technical complexity in a simple way. The metaphor used was the light bulb being turned on in a darkened room. One day the switch would flip to "on" and I would fully understand. My growing awareness of how sexism impacted Hillary's presidential campaign wasn't achieved as easily as a switch turning on; it was a slow rotation, as with a dimmer switch. With each incremental turn, a cultural undercurrent that involved women and presidential politics was illuminated. It changed me profoundly.

The first turn of that political dimmer switch happened in my kitchen in 2007. I was watching Hillary's online announcement to the nation that she was running for president. In the video, sitting on a couch and looking into the camera, she said, "I'm beginning a conversation with you, with America."

I had never heard of anyone announcing a presidential run in such an understated way, and it felt awkward. There was no man on a stage with his wife dutifully standing next to him to project an image of family. There was no mention of God. It was just her, alone, and she wanted to talk about our country. She wanted to "chat." The image of her looking back at me was unique.

That metaphorical dimmer switch turned up one millimeter.

The next event was in January of 2008. It was the evening of the first primary election in the much-anticipated Iowa caucus. (Iowa, at this point, was one of only four states that had never elected a woman to any national office.) I was watching Chris Matthews on the MSNBC news show *Hardball,* as I always did. Hillary had come in third in the caucus, and it was a shocker, as she had been expected to win. Matthews was full of bravado as he questioned whether Hillary should stay in the race. That hit me in my gut. Why would a pundit suggest she should quit at the start of the primaries? After all, both Bill Clinton and George W. Bush lost Iowa's coveted first place win when they ran for the presidency. I didn't remember people calling for them to quit the race.

Another millimeter.

Then on the heels of the Iowa loss was her New Hampshire win. That night, I got my daughter out of bed, and we watched Hillary's victory speech together. I said to her, "She is going to be our next president." That was odd. I had never said those words before.

I could feel that dimmer switch turning up another millimeter.

But something happened the next day on *Hardball* that would continue to happen on many shows after every state Hillary won. Chris Matthews looked glum on the news panel of reporters and commentators who were discussing Hillary's New Hampshire win, when he remarked, "the reason she may be a front-runner is her husband messed around. That's how she got to be senator from New York." He said it confidently, as if he were declaring a fact, somehow sure that a woman could never win a presidential primary or a U.S. Senate race on her own merit without voter sympathy about a cheating husband. This dislike and, often times, hatred for her by liberal progressives was something for which I was naively unprepared. I expected the venom to be delivered by Republicans and conservative pundits, but not from her supposed allies.

The sexualization of women who dare enter the male halls of authority is a common tactic to suppress female ambitions for the White House. And men aren't the only ones who resort to it. When the liberal Air America radio show host Randi Rhodes called Hillary a "big fucking whore" and another Air America host, Stephanie Miller, continually referred to Hillary as "Mrs. Clinton" instead of Senator Clinton, these subtle and not-so-subtle attacks succeeded in doing two things: They relegated Hillary to a mere sexual being, and they erased her substantive political experience, both as United States senator and as First Lady.

Plenty of examples of that abound. Conservative MSNBC host Tucker Carlson said in July of 2007, "She scares me. I cross my legs every time she talks." When discussing Hillary's performance at one of the debates, MSNBC commentator Mike Barnicle said Hillary's attitude made her "... [look] like everyone's first wife standing outside a probate court." This created a bonding moment for the all male panel, as they laughed at that image comparing a serious presidential candidate to that of an annoying spouse.

Another millimeter.

The Hillary hate was also marketed. When the Hillary Clinton nutcracker came along in 2008, it was advertised with the feature of "serrated stainless steel thighs that, well, crack nuts." That, coupled with Tucker's revelation, should have clued me in to the pairing of men and Oval Office politics as a clubhouse that had a "No Girls Allowed" sign hanging on the door.

At the time, I was a daily listener to National Public Radio and a reader of progressive blogs, but their common use of sports analogies awakened my senses to a different way of interpreting political coverage. NPR correspondents would open news shows with biased lines about Obama inching closer to Hillary's delegate count with phrases such as, "He's within striking distance." *Daily Kos* bloggers wrote articles about the state primary dates with themes that reflected a boxing game "... the DNC put a stop to these contests, thwarting her ability to land a knockout punch here."

Why care about sports analogies? Because they are common in our traditionally male presidential campaign history. Reporters use sports symbolism to cover a race more easily; policy issues are complex, and contests are simple. When women enter races, they are expected to be one of the guys and participate in the language of sports, but that is a man's game. Men have been building campaign traditions since the founding of this country. By boiling down the primary race into a sports contest, of sorts, it repudiated Hillary's solid experience—a major experience difference between her and Obama and a suggestion that to win, she needed to "be one of the boys."

I could see that a powerful male context was flowing through American presidential politics. The dimmer switch about how male-oriented our political system was turning up full force but wasn't yet on all the way. However, the building blocks of our nation's politics were in greater view for me.

When my progressive friends offered that their line in the sand with Hillary was her Senate vote for the Iraq War Resolution, I noted that there had been no similar line in the sand for John Kerry in 2004 or for Senator Joe Biden when he was nominated as Obama's vice presidential running mate in 2008. Both of these men voted for the Iraq War. This revelation was usually met with silence.

The dimmer switch was a millimeter away from full.

I also came to realize that a presidential nominee has to be likable and, alternately, an aggressor. This is easier for men to portray than for women because of historical archetypes. For the first time we saw a First Lady—the most traditional of political mother images—run for president, and people had to take the Norman Rockwell ideal of a fatherly leader of our nation who sometimes reluctantly declares war and replace it with a motherly image of a woman. In Hillary's case, she was both a mother and senator who voted for the Iraq War Resolution. This is a combination of two archetypes, caregiver and ruler. For many, this created chaos.

With all the gendered criticism of her, as well as a reluctance to acknowledge her experience and qualifications, I stopped listening to Air America, NPR, and Chris Matthews. I un-book-marked the *Daily Kos*. Within a few months I even discontinued my cable service. I had to re-think everything I believed about partisan politics.

I found the hatred for Hillary interesting because I thought that progressives would have been proud of Clinton's experience as First Lady, notably her speech to the Fourth World Conference on Women in 1995 in Beijing. At that now-famous event, Hillary made a high-profile speech about global women's rights that included the now oft-quoted line, "Human rights are women's rights and women's rights are human rights." She spoke passionately about the fact that even though there are many people who would try to silence the words of women on issues concerning the human rights of women and girls, that freedom of speech on these issues was extremely important.

Prior to her trip, the White House administration was nervous about China's reaction to her speech, especially as she singled out that country's silencing of women. She ignored their fear and proceeded with her plan. Her speech sent positive shock waves across the globe and was met with tremendous applause by both liberals and conservatives. Looking back now we can see how forward-thinking her speech was on policy issues for women. It was the perfect blend of two images: leader and mother.

A few people angrily asked me why Clinton didn't quit the race for president, as they thought she was standing in the way of Obama. I think what they really wanted to know was why I wasn't quitting Hillary. Now the dimmer switch was turned up to full because I had to answer this for myself. And, this is where my shift in understanding took place. It was June of 2008, and it was the end of the primary race.

My old hallmarks of progressivism that formed part of my identity had dissolved, and I saw partisan politics more objectively. I had developed a new way of looking at the political world, especially with regard to women. All the writers, anchors, and politicians just looked like a deck of cards to me. In my mind I took the deck, placed it between my thumb and forefinger, and jettisoned the cards into the air. I didn't look to see where the cards fell because I had already walked through the political looking glass. I was in the wilderness. I felt alone, and it was just a little bit cold. But in reality, I was with eighteen million voters who stayed with her, those cracks in the male ceiling of the Oval Office. We could all see differently now after having experienced that campaign.

Hillary's presence and words were a powerful message to girls and women, and that is why she didn't quit. And as a mother of a daughter, that is one of the reasons I didn't quit her. To be sure, Hillary was fighting to win, but she also knew that we needed the memory and the images to move forward for those who came after her. Like her Beijing speech, she was ahead of the curve, but this was a rougher road. The accusations that were hurled at Hillary were hurled at all of us. We were all called "bitter clingers," "vagina voters," "working class," "old," and "bitches" right along with her and suffered the same dismissal as she did. And some of the people who threw out those slurs were feminists.

Hillary's 2008 campaign is now a snapshot that is a part of our collective cultural memory from past events that we all share. These memories help us form our identities as individuals and as citizens. Boys and men have the totality of presidential cultural memory reflected to them in the United States: Franklin D. Roosevelt holding up his hat, Dwight Eisenhower with arms held aloft, and John F. Kennedy with Marilyn Monroe. The history of male presidents is the gendered bedrock of power upon which we form our national identity, and women, without similar memories, sense their lack of power.

I grieved when Hillary lost the nomination. The night after she won in South Dakota, one of the last primary states in a campaign already lost, I dreamt about her.

In the dream, Hillary was in the White House. I was with many women in a room waiting to meet with her. When it was my turn, Hillary stood in front of me. I held out my arms as if to receive something. She placed several Middle Eastern shawls and fabrics into my empty arms. I knew women had made them. I took them.

Several years later after the election, I finished my film about the women's liberation movement and started to speak about how important it is to remember that movement and include it in our cultural memory. If we had had a cultural memory about female leaders in 2008, Hillary may not have been seen as an interloper in the male Oval Office.

As soon as I released my film in 2013, I received an invitation to screen it in Islamabad, Pakistan, as a guest of the International Islamic University. Was I afraid to go? Yes. But after having lived through the 2008 presidential campaign, complete with its gendered rhetoric and undercurrent of dismissiveness of women, I knew how important it was for me to go. Hillary gave me the strength, and I traveled alone.

I screened my film and spoke to an amazing group of Pakistani women who were in the midst of shaping feminism in their own country and wanted to learn more about American feminism. Later, with several of these Pakistani women, I went shopping in one of their open markets. I bought some beautiful fabrics, and as I took them in my arms, I remembered the dream and remembered that Hillary also had been to Pakistan.

That dream wasn't about me personally. Nor was the 2008 campaign just about the loss of my preferred candidate. There was a bigger picture developing here, and it was an image of Americans connecting with women in faraway places from the symbolic power of a woman in the Oval Office in a way that can't happen if we elect another man to the White House.

I know Hillary is a big part of this picture. I can see that clearly now because the lights are turned up brightly.

Without Hillary Clinton, What Would Conservatives Have to Write About?

Emily Zanotti

Hillary Clinton is responsible for me having a successful writing career.

I don't mean that in the typical way, of course. As a dedicated Libertarian, my committed opposition for nearly every policy proposal and principled stand Hillary Clinton has taken in her lifetime is well-recorded and easily demonstrated. I'm not in the village it takes to raise a child. I am squarely in the opposition camp in the War on Women—at least, so I've heard. And given the opportunity to pick my own feminist anthem, I'll go with the one written by Ayn Rand.

But even I'm big enough to admit that when a woman breaks a glass ceiling, she takes more than just her own colleagues and followers with her. In this case, while climbing the ladder to national prominence, not only has Hillary Clinton paved the way for powerful women on both sides of the aisle to enter the upper echelons of government, but she's created (and has maintained) an insatiable appetite for conservative commentary.

You could rightfully call Hillary's entrance into the public eye the Pantsuit Advent. Before her, a First Lady with a national policy agenda unrelated to the introduction of French food or starting a national conversation about the propriety of informal hat wearing was almost unheard of. As presidential contenders, the Clintons were a two-fer, and Mrs. Clinton did not take her departure from the White House as the end of her career. She entered public life on her own, earned a spot in the U.S. Senate, and launched the kind of laudable political career that any heavy-hitting statesman would envy. And many do: that envy has driven women on both sides of the aisle ever further, whether they're looking to be the "next Hillary Clinton," or to be the woman so powerful that she relegates Hillary to the back part of the history book typically reserved for America's most influential political craftspeople.

She is the reason that Republicans welcomed Sarah Palin into their loving embrace, regardless of whether Hillary herself considers that an achievement. She's the reason that nomination short-lists today are full of female presidential contenders. She's the reason that any female seeking elected office receives serious consideration. It may be the play of demographics—after all, fulfilling quotas is far from real feminism—but forward movement toward fair representation, no matter what's fueling it, is a marked success. It may, for unfortunate Republicans, yield a few decades of women who fit the preferred stereotype, but in the long run, a little feminine influence on the party of old white dudes could go a very long way. I mean, even some white wine in those cigar-smoke-filled back rooms would be an improvement.

But inspiring legions of conservative women to enter the political ring in order to fight Hillary Clinton's influence on global politics is not the only way that Hillary has impacted my career options. After all, people only enter politics when they're literally unhirable in any other field. I can say, with complete confidence, that Hillary Clinton is mostly responsible for the market which sustains me: the appetite for conservative writing.

It may not seem that way, but this is a testament to Hillary's ability to successfully make such a mark on her opposition that she lives rent-free in their heads for decades. Many politicians can comfortably lay claim to the idea that they've gotten under their opponents' skin. Barack Obama, for example, has tortured the sentiments of second-rate talking heads for his entire term in office, some of whom lay awake at night, still wondering whether they can prove his supposed Kenyan heritage in order to force the poor African nation to take him back. But few can claim to eat away at the hearts and souls of opposing forces for decades, burrowing into their brains and tearing, little by little, at the fabric that holds together the precious remains of their sanity like Hillary Clinton. Nearly every action taken in politics post-1992 has earned a comparison to the Clinton way of doing things. Virtually every political commentator, op-ed columnist, and book writer has, at one time or another, asked themselves, "What Would Hillary Do?" and, in the absence of better fodder, penned a thousand words on the subject.

And the appetite for this sort of thing is growing. The first successful *New York Times* bestselling conservative books that employed humor as a vehicle rather than the dry, complicated pronouncements of high-level economics and political theory, hit bookshelves during the Clinton administration. Authors regaled a waiting public with half-true tales of smashed table lamps, missing files, and silk Shantung pantsuit collections. They interviewed "former Secret Service agents" and employed gossip columnists to opine on the state of White House intimate relations. They chattered on about whether Socks the Cat's thoughts could be translated, and whether Chelsea Clinton, once old enough to rebel against her parents, could be persuaded to pen a tell-all and a *Lifetime* movie.

And a career was born.

Now, I'm not saying that my career is entirely the result of Clinton-era machinations, but I'd be hard-pressed to believe that the rise of the conservative blogger, and the conservative opinion columnist, and the conservative gossip magnate, and the conservative best-selling author, would be possible if the Clintons hadn't inspired the existing conservative media to become like Joan Rivers on the Academy Awards red carpet (back when the late Joan Rivers was the unforgiving red carpet matriarch).

And so, Hillary Clinton opens yet another door for a group she never expected to inspire.

In seriousness, regardless of political affiliation, the rise of the powerful, influential stateswoman is an achievement for everyone. History is peppered with only a few remarkable women who have achieved global notoriety and who have made significant strides in leadership. They're all immediately recognizable: Margaret Thatcher, Golda Meir, Indira Gandhi, Eleanor Roosevelt; some even just by their first names—Oprah—but regardless of where they stand on the political spectrum, they've all had a significant effect on what it's like to grow up as a girl in the twenty-first century.

Hillary Clinton, despite all assurances to the contrary from my ideologically identical countrymen, can confidently include herself in that group. Growing up a girl in America is to know her name, agree with her policies or not. And frankly, we're better for it.

Can Hillary Clinton Count on the Gen Y Vote?

Jolie Hunsinger

Social media obsessed. Shortcut takers. Self-entitled. These are just a few of the stigmas my generation has been given. But look deeper. My peers, the twenty-somethings currently making their way into the workforce, are slowly moving mountains. Breaking molds. We are a generation of diversity-tolerant individuals who are generally accepting of mindsets and lifestyles that, even five or ten years ago, were frowned upon or considered unacceptable by the generations before us. We have adopted an equal opportunity opinion of differences in race and gender in hopes that pairing those terms with "minority" will soon be a thing of the past.

Today, women outnumber men not only on college campuses earning their master's degrees, but also in careers such as law, medicine, and business. Jobs that were previously dominated by men are now strongly represented by female contenders. For example, my graduating class from veterinary school in 2014 was nearly 80 percent women. In the early 1990s, this career was still predominantly viewed as "men's work," and women entering the field were considered to be too weak to handle the rigor associated with the tasks they needed to perform. Women are closing the gender gap and becoming tomorrow's leaders. So why is it that a woman has yet to take presidential office? When it comes to whether it's time to see a woman in the Oval Office, Hillary Clinton put it best when she said, "It is past time for women to take their rightful place, side by side with men, in the rooms where the fates of peoples, where their children's and grandchildren's fates, are decided."

And I'm more than ready for that to happen.

The year 2008 was the first year I was eligible to vote for a presidential candidate. I was excited that my vote, the voice of an admittedly awkward twenty-year-old, might play a part in making history if Hillary Clinton were elected to the White House. While most of my newbie voter excitement was directed toward getting a woman into that office, I also supported Hillary for many of the reasons I still do today. For starters, she avidly supported public schools. Having completed my elementary and high school educations in the public school system, I was (and still am) familiar with how funding can play a role in the quality of education one receives. Sure, the basic subjects like math and English will always be covered, but programs like art and music are constantly the victims of budget cuts despite the fact that these programs allow students to develop individuality and express their talents. Growing up in a low- to middle-income community, I admired Clinton's opinions on cutting taxes for those with lower incomes. Even in the middle of my undergraduate education, I knew I had chosen a career that would not guarantee me a spot in the coveted financial "upper class." Sure, I knew I'd be able to make a living, but voting for a candidate that supported fairer taxation was a no-brainer for me.

Before she announced her candidacy, it felt like everyone's attention was focused on Clinton's State Department email "scandal" instead of looking at what her future plans were for the country. What was probably a move on her part to simplify her hectic life turned into what the media loves—the perfect, juicy, pre-campaign debacle. While I understand that media coverage must include both a candidate's viewpoints on the hot-button issues and any potential political missteps, we must not forget that politicians, like us, are human. Mistakes happen. We, as I am sure Clinton is doing, take note to not make the same mistakes again and move on to the next tasks at hand. Clinton gets a high five from me for handling the supposed scandal with poise and not allowing the incident to mar her confidence.

Fast-forward to today. I have completed eight years of college and doctoral programs in total. I have my first job in the real world, and I am saddled with a nauseating amount of student debt. Not only am I worried about how I'm going to pay it off or just how long that will take, but also I'm concerned that if I ever have children, their debt load will be even deeper than mine. That being said, at this point in my life, my radar is set to locate a presidential candidate who is willing to work toward lowering the cost of a college education and help relieve the current student debt load. Clinton's work with the College Cost Reduction and Access Act has helped lower loan payments to allow new graduates to achieve their aspirations with less worry, myself included.

In order for my generation, tomorrow's leaders, to thrive in today's society, we need a president with an open mind that can adapt with the ever-changing viewpoints of a more and more unprejudiced people. We also need someone who is strong-willed, someone who can stand their ground when faced with opposition and adversity. Hillary Clinton has proven that she is able to weather political storms as evidenced by her roles as First Lady, U.S. senator, and secretary of state. Additionally, Clinton has demonstrated interest and voted in favor of some of the hot topics important to my generation, such as the environment, gay rights, and women's rights. With Clinton in office, progress on these issues and more can, and will, be made.

As Clinton put it, "If a country doesn't recognize minority rights and human rights, including women's rights, you will not have the kind of stability and prosperity that is possible."

As I look around, it's evident to me that women are increasing their presence in government, as business leaders, and as dedicated employees. With Clinton as president, women's rights in the workplace and equal pay will become more of a priority on Capitol Hill than it's ever been before. I have no doubt that she will fight until that infamous glass ceiling is shattered, and it is my sincerest hope that my children will know nothing of gender inequality because of the work yet to be done by Hillary Clinton and other future presidents.

I'm sure I speak for my Generation Y colleagues when I say it's time to shake things up. By checking off Hillary Clinton's name on my ballot next November, I believe I'll be choosing progress not only for current generations, but for generations yet to come. It's time for someone to fight for women's rights, destroy minority labels, and forge paths for a healthier, happier United States.

So check that box; join Hillary and my generation. It's time to break some molds.

Hillary for President . . . of the Universe

Sally Kohn

In an interview with *New York Magazine*, her first after leaving the State Department, Hillary Clinton began her public flirtation with running for president. "I will just continue to weigh what the factors are that would influence me making a decision one way or the other," Clinton said. The day the interview came out, the United Nations General Assembly opened in New York City. Coincidence? I think not! It's a sign. But for me, Hillary Clinton would be better off running for President of the Universe. Actually, she doesn't even have to run. Let's just appoint her. Who would complain?

After all, as the 2016 campaign moves forward, more and more voters are disillusioned with the disappointing and self-destructive centrism of President Barack Obama. They may start to remember that he's simply regurgitating the Clintonian politics of timid triangulation with which Hillary and her husband helped poison the political waters. If, following an economic crash that Bill Clinton's policies of deregulation helped to, in large part, precipitate, Obama bafflingly appointed the same crowd of economic lackeys to clean up the mess (Larry Summers, Tim Geithner, etc.), do we somehow think Hillary would become the hold-Wall-Street-accountable force that Obama has failed to be? Not likely. More likely is that Hillary, arguably more deeply embedded within Wall Street and big business circles than President Obama ever was to begin with, would continue the soft policies of economic liberalism that tinker around the edges of inequality while quietly shoring up corporate power. She's given us little indication she would do otherwise.

In his very thoughtful *Daily Beast* essay, "The Rise of the New New Left," Peter Beinart argues that younger Americans are moving away from politics as circumscribed by Ronald Reagan and reified, with little amendment, by Bill Clinton. Bill Clinton, you'll remember, was the guy who proudly proclaimed, "The era of big government is over." Beinart cites a 2010 Pew Research poll that found that two-thirds of younger Americans favor a bigger government with more services over a cheaper government with fewer services—a margin of support "25 points above the rest of the population." And 74 percent of 18- to 29-year-olds believe that "a free market economy needs government regulation in order to best serve the public interest," compared with just 57 percent of seniors. Now who was it again who slashed government regulations of the economy?

Then there's Hillary's dogged support for the war in Iraq, an unpopular choice among Democratic voters and, increasingly, all Americans. Or her ambivalent-at-best support for immigrant rights in New York State. Or her mushy views on preserving entitlements like Social Security. Remember, in 2008, one of Barack Obama's attack lines against Hillary was that she was "trying to sound or vote like Republicans."

The American people overwhelmingly support tough accountability for Wall Street and aggressive solutions to unemployment and inequality. We need a president who stands with the people.

I'm not saying that faced with a Republican alternative who is even cozier with Wall Street and even less inclined to repair our frayed social safety net and prioritize yawning economic inequality, Hillary Clinton might not look like a shimmering example of social justice. But the reality is that many voters, especially the rising generation, will be holding their noses and pulling the lever. Rather than a further retrenchment in Clinton-era austerity politics and anti-government cuts, it would be nice to have a bold and fresh alternative. But one can't emerge if Hillary doesn't step aside—and to do so, she would need a better offer. Ruler of the world sounds promising....

Now I'm aware, as some have accused, that my criticism of Ms. Clinton may either bolster other sexism-inspired critiques or, on its own, reeks of sexism. Maybe. Is it, for instance, inherently sexist to wrap up Hillary Clinton's ideology with that of her husband—in a way that no one probably would if the genders were reversed? Perhaps. Is it biased of me to deride not only Hillary's policy stances but her personality—that, for instance, my gripe isn't just with her Wall Street-friendly economic vision but her utter failure to convey an ounce of warm and caring populist concern? Possibly.

But to be fair, I don't think (for instance) that Elizabeth Warren is the greatest public speaker in the universe nor is she gifted with near the same levels of charisma possessed by Barack Obama or Ronald Reagan, and yet I can overlook that because I think her policy vision is spot-on. And yes, I can sometimes give Obama a pass on his über-centrism because of his buckets full of charisma. But when both policy and personality are lacking, it's hard to find something to cheer for. If Hillary Clinton becomes the Democratic nominee for president in 2016, make no mistake about it, I will cheer for her. But if Hillary wants me to cheer more enthusiastically, she'll have to start championing a more progressive vision. Or bow out to liberal candidates whose vision and passion are more in line with the populist sentiments—and needs—of America at this moment.

Still, Hillary is too great a talent and voice to go unused. And she clearly has too much fight and force left in her to just follow the fading path of philanthropy laid out by her husband. Plus if Hillary showed us nothing else, it's her extraordinary vision and impact as a global statesman. Which is precisely what we need in the world right now, a strong head of a strong global body that can collectively hold rogue nations accountable and spread opportunity and prosperity worldwide, like the United Nations if the U.N. had even more accountability and heft and teeth. Added bonus to being president of the universe: Taking such a position would help breathe life into the perennial vast right-wing conspiracy theory about "world government," and we know how Hillary likes vast right-wing conspiracies!

Hillary has already visited an insane number of countries during her tenure as secretary of state, so she could ostensibly phone it in for the first few years of her global presidency. Plus— let's be honest—since most Americans probably don't know many of those countries exist, let alone where to find them on a map, Hillary's prodigious global knowledge would be wasted on our domestic electorate. Hillary describes her own tenure at State this way: "I thought it was essential that as we restore America's standing in the world and strengthen our global leadership again, we needed what I took to calling 'smart power' to elevate American diplomacy and development and reposition them for the twenty-first century." By the same token, there is clearly a need to restore Kenya and Indonesia and Mexico's standing in the world, too, and expand development and opportunity there and in countless other places. In particular, a global Hillary "presidency" would do much to empower women and girls worldwide, both in symbolic and tangible ways through investment projects, a strategic way to improve development standards for all. Not to mention the fact that Hillary Clinton is the most admired woman *in the world*. In fact, she has been for the last 13 years.

Time to capitalize on that global popularity, Hillary. Ideally, the United States would decisively throw out the bad bathwater of the last 20 years of Reagan/Clinton/Bush economics and not put another Clinton (or Bush) in the White House. But there's no need to throw the baby out with the bathwater, or "to put baby in a corner." Hillary Clinton is a global star and a beacon for positive values and change worldwide. Here's hoping she sets her political sights even higher! Symbolic figurehead-like world domination—with no actual economic policy power, please.

An earlier version of this essay originally appeared at The Daily Beast.

A Yankee in a Southern Belle's Court

Suzi Parker

Hillary Rodham Clinton appeared on my radar at a young age. That's because she arrived in my home state of Arkansas as a brazen Yankee Yale graduate when I was five years old and turned it upside down. She may have been a young woman in love with an Arkansas boy, but she wasn't a Southern belle interested in lady luncheons at the country club. Hillary had another agenda, and it was much more than being just another political wife.

She wanted to be a force.

She fully splashed onto the landscape and the front pages of my state's two daily newspapers when her husband ran for Arkansas attorney general in 1976. She looked nothing like other political wives in the state, preferring makeup-free skin to a Merle Norman mask. Her massive hooty owl glasses covering her face made her look serious, studious, and anything but sexy. Arkansas women shuddered at what they perceived as her lack of womanliness in their bows-and-blush world.

She didn't care. Why should she? Even in high school in Illinois, she was referred to as "Sister Frigidaire," and as an undergraduate at the prestigious all-woman's Wellesley College, she intimidated her peers, according to a 1993 *New Yorker* profile on the Clintons. In the land of moonlight, magnolias, and sugary sweetness, she was seen as a feminist carpetbagger who had unfairly snatched an eligible bachelor from beauty queens.

That image set the stage for Hillary's tumultuous time in Arkansas.

For a young girl growing up in a perceived backward Southern state in the 1970s, Hillary couldn't have landed at a better time. The fight for the Equal Rights Amendment, which appeared on the news, might as well have been happening on another planet. I saw women marching in New York City, but they certainly weren't marching with signs of protest in Pine Bluff, Arkansas. Every woman I knew was married and few worked outside the home. In Hillary, I saw an independent, determined career woman who had her own life and wasn't going to abandon it for her husband. And I wasn't the only one who noticed that she was, indeed, a force.

"I first met Hillary when she moved to Fayetteville to work in Bill's Congressional campaign before joining the law school faculty," said Stephen Smith, a law professor at the University of Arkansas who also worked on Bill Clinton's early campaigns. "I was immediately impressed with her intelligence, discipline, and sardonic wit, and I admired that she was both forthright and unafraid."

While Bill Clinton took over the Attorney General's post at the State Capitol in Little Rock, Hillary started work at the prestigious Rose Law Firm, the oldest law firm west of the Mississippi. The only lawyers I knew, like my godfather, were white males. In 1979, the year that Clinton became governor, Hillary became the firm's first female partner. Around that time, I started pondering a law career, perhaps subconsciously influenced by Hillary.

Everyone I knew seemed to be talking about Hillary. During my mother's weekly hair appointment at the beauty shop, women discussed the blandness of Hillary's look. How dare she be caught in a photograph not looking "dolled up"? Those glasses needed to go. And her hair? The hair needed to go also—too plain Jane.

At the coffee shop on Saturdays where my father met a group of men, Hillary's ambition often popped up in conversation. Some men appeared confused by her determination; others in the legal know said she was one of the best lawyers—if not the best—in the state.

But always on the front burner was the fact that Hillary was not one of us. She wasn't Southern. She didn't talk with a drawl. She didn't play coy. She didn't mince words. She possessed raw motivation, and she didn't hide it behind a girly giggle and fluttering eyelashes. And those were the things that fascinated me about this Yankee fish out of water. I wasn't the only one who noticed those things.

"The thing I'm always struck by is not only how alien she must have seemed to most Arkansans but also how alien they must have seemed to her," said Janine Parry, a political science professor at the University of Arkansas.

Hillary's name—or lack of her husband's surname—constantly presented a problem. When she married Bill Clinton in 1975, Hillary chose to keep "Rodham" as her professional name and shockingly passed on the traditional route of adopting her husband's last name. While that was an increasingly common decision for women in the 1970s in other parts of the country, that move, in a Bible Belt state where women were often taught in church to obey their husbands, did not play well politically. In his first Democratic primary, opponents made Hillary's name a campaign issue.

As a 1994 *New Yorker* article pointed out: "One friend recalled standing next to her at a reception at the Rose firm in the late seventies, and seeing a man approach her, jab angrily at the name tag pinned to her blouse, and fairly spit out, 'That's not your name!'"

As a proper young girl growing up in Arkansas then, it was

refreshing and liberating to me that Hillary had chosen to remain seen as an independent woman separate from her marriage. It was a decision that, according to Bill Clinton in that same *New Yorker* article, Hillary made at the age of nine. My mother had wanted to do that, but in 1957, when she married, such a choice would have been seen as beyond subversive. Image did matter when my mother was a bride, and apparently not much had changed in Arkansas more than twenty years later.

Many people, including close Clinton friends, partly blamed Bill Clinton's only reelection loss in 1980 on Hillary's refusal to take his name. Always the strategist, Hillary later did tack "Clinton" on to her own name and caved more to the softer side of Southern life, perfecting the gaze of the perfect Southern political wife, lightening her hair, and foregoing the glasses for contacts. I hated her for those changes.

That was the start of my long love-hate relationship with Hillary.

* * *

While I had met Bill Clinton in third grade on a field trip to the State Capitol, Hillary was more elusive. I knew a lot about her because my father worked in circles that included Hillary. He painted her as an arrogant, tough-as-nails bossy woman in meetings. He wasn't exactly a fan.

Still, that kind of attitude enchanted me as a teenager. My mother possessed a similar demeanor in that she was a strong woman who took no prisoners, but she had not attended college. Hillary, of course, had.

One day when I was in high school, my mother and I were shopping in Little Rock at a downtown mall. Suddenly, in a store, Hillary appeared with her young daughter, Chelsea, who, like all little girls around the age of seven, wanted her mother to buy her something. Hillary was having none of that. She whipped around and quickly told Chelsea that she didn't need whatever it was and that they had to go. She paid no attention to my mother and me standing within earshot and observing her parenting skills. I quickly soured on the notion of Hillary. While I don't know what had been going on between mother and daughter in the minutes leading up to the scene I witnessed; in that moment she was harsher than I ever imagined.

A few weeks later, I spotted Bill shopping with Chelsea in a popular Little Rock department store. He let Chelsea help him pick out suits and ties and genuinely listened to his daughter's choices. It provided a stark contrast to Hillary's behavior, and an insight, however brief, into the lives of who were to become the world's most famous political couple. My love for Hillary returned in 1990, when her actions topped the six o'clock news. In a grand spectacular fashion at the State Capitol, during Bill Clinton's reelection campaign for governor, she ambushed his Democratic primary opponent, Tom McRae, and seized his press conference. It was the gutsiest move I had ever seen by a high-profile woman—or perhaps even a man—in Arkansas.

McRae, who was the great-grandson of a former Arkansas governor, decided to hold a press conference while Bill Clinton was out of the state. Behind McRae hung a caricature of a naked Bill. His hands were strategically placed, and the phrase "The emperor has no clothes" was written on the backdrop. He began his press conference, and a female voice interrupted loudly, "Do you really want an answer, Tom?"

There was Hillary, who said later she just happened to be in the capital. Of course, it was accidental (wink, wink). Hillary continued to explain to the press there how her husband couldn't give him an answer because he was in Washington, D.C., on state business performing the job the people of Arkansas elected him to do. "That sounds a bit like a stunt to me," she said, according to newspaper archives.

Some people balked at her brassiness. One editorial said that

that Hillary moment signaled a changing of the times in the Old South, and it wasn't for the best. The author wrote, "It was only further evidence that Southerners are at last becoming totally modern, fully Americanized and unabashedly advanced. For some reason, the news does not please."

For many, though, the legendary hellcat Hillary publically emerging was beautifully brash. She emasculated McRae in a cool, calm, combative fashion that made many young women in Arkansas realize that they had a voice and, more importantly, could use it. It certainly influenced me to the point that even now, twenty-five years later, when I get mad I often say, "I'm about to have a Hillary-McRae moment."

One year later, Arkansas had to share its fiery First Lady with the world when Bill Clinton decided to run for president. Many people were happy to see Hillary go, but they all knew that Arkansas would never be the same. Hillary had accomplished what she intended, skyrocketing a stuck Southern state into the modern era. But she was forever changed, too. As she said in a 2007 interview with the *Concord Monitor*, "Moving to Arkansas and living there for 18 years was probably the most important formative set of experiences that I had for what I'm doing now."

✳ ✳ ✳

I still have a love-hate relationship with Hillary. Some days, I really love her when she is fearlessly taking on someone like Rand Paul. Other days, when she is trying too hard to be the perfect people-pleasing politician, I strongly dislike her. Ultimately, however, I have to give Hillary credit for being a critical role model in my life.

Hillary showed me—and many other women—that with hard work, keen wits, and savvy smarts, you could break glass ceilings. And if somehow things didn't work out, we should keep at it until that ceiling cracks. While she may have briefly caved to the ways of the Southern woman with bleached hair and a softer image, she nevertheless proved that she wasn't some little woman standing by her man. Hillary has always made it clear that the choices she makes are her own decisions, and that remains a valuable lesson for women.

Hillary Clinton: Everymother
Linda Lowen

What kind of mother is Hillary Clinton? I don't care, and neither should you.

No man has ever made his mark as a great dad first . . . and, oh yeah, a world leader second. How Hillary raised Chelsea is a topic that's never concerned me. With two daughters of my own, I've spent enough time churning the angsty stew of maternal self-doubt to worry about anyone else, let alone Hillary. What matters to me is Hillary's impact on the generation of girls and young women who witnessed her first run for president: the successes, the confidence, the backlash, the defeat. She showed the world that an earnest, hardworking, capable female could be taken seriously, that women have value beyond their looks.

✳ ✳ ✳

The smart girl with glasses who went to a women's college—that described Hillary and that described me. My affection for her stems from a common core of experience. But in the process of raising my girls, it hardened into love. Women of achievement are uncommon enough that each one serves as a role model. Hillary stands above them all as proof that a woman can accomplish nearly anything. We've paid lip service to that pipe dream for years, but during the heady 17 months of her 2008 campaign, Hillary inspired little girls to switch their career aspirations from Princess to President.

Hillary is the archetypal Powerful Female who lets no man subjugate her. Despite the humiliation of her husband's infidelity, she carried on with courage, conviction, strength, and fortitude, moving beyond scandal to build a life independent of Bill. She rose to power at a critical time in my girls' lives, setting an example I could never hope to match. I feel so indebted I've considered sending her a Mother's Day card. If I had the nerve, I'd write: *Thanks for easing the burden on me. I didn't need to try to be Superwoman to show my daughters that it could be done. In your pantsuit and pageboy, you already had that covered.*

My daughters are in their twenties now, but in the summer of 2007, my daughters were deeply impacted by Hillary's run for the White House. Jaye was sixteen, Em was thirteen, and the fair was coming to town. An annual event that attracts close to a million visitors each year, the New York State Fair is always held in Syracuse, our hometown. For eleven days straddling August and September, the Fair becomes the epicenter of all activity in the state, including political campaigns. At the Fair, small acts have big repercussions. It's been said that Hillary sealed her first Senate win by eating a big, greasy Gianelli sausage sandwich—a Fair favorite. Presumably to keep his trim figure camera-ready, her opponent refused—and lost.

Although I have no plans to run for anything, I always eat a sausage sandwich every year. My daughters had their own rituals, starting with a candy apple and an all-day unlimited-ride wristband to the Midway. But that year, as rebellious teens, they abandoned ritual for revolution.

In early July, Em announced, "Projekt Revolution is going to play the Grandstand! My Chemical Romance is part of the lineup!"

Knowing that was her favorite band, I tried to head her off at the pass. "Forget it. You're 13."

"I'll be turning 14 three weeks after that! This could be my birthday present. And Jaye can come too."

"I'm not letting you two go to the concert alone. It's miles away. What would you do if something happened?"

"Mom, you'll be within walking distance! It's on the same day you're working for Hillary at the fair!"

She had me at Hillary. I'd signed up to staff Senator Clinton's presidential campaign booth from 10 a.m. to 10 p.m. The all-day concert would start at noon, wrap up by eleven, and I'd be less than an eighth of a mile away the whole time. God Save the Senator.

Hillary never knew she did them a solid, but my daughters never forgot. Already on their way to being feminists, they became staunch Hillary supporters. I'd sown the seeds years ago, and it was only a matter of time. Our home held book-shelves lined with *The Case for Hillary Clinton* by Susan Estrich, *Hillary's Choice* by Gail Sheehy, *The Girls on the Van: Covering Hillary* by Beth Harpaz. Our front lawn sprouted campaign signs proclaiming Hillary for Senate and Hillary for President. Our bank account had grown thanks to paychecks courtesy of Hillary, albeit indirectly; as a writer, radio/TV producer, and Internet blogger covering women's issues, I made a living off of what she said and did during the 2008 election cycle. Our world revolved around Hillary, and the girls thought this was normal.

Outside our family, the Hillary haters tried to set my daughters straight. Never shy about talking politics—a trait I proudly claim responsibility for—Jaye tried to debate the merits of the candidates with friends. As the tide of public opinion turned toward Barack Obama, Jaye reported she was often shouted down. Some even said, "Just shut up about Hillary. Nobody wants a woman for president."

Misogyny or sniping—does it matter? Judging women's lives has always been a blood sport. Hillary's 2008 campaign drew fire, but she was the first truly viable female presidential candidate. Previously, if women graced the political stage, they did so as sidekick, gracious helpmate, shiny ornament hanging from the executive branch of power. Whether they sparkled or shattered depended on optics. Hillary's first joint interview with Bill during his 1992 presidential campaign was essentially no different. A well-planned offensive intended to deflect Gennifer Flowers' claim that she'd had an ongoing affair with Bill, the interview aired on *60 Minutes*. Largely silent and nodding agreeably during much of the Q&A with correspondent Steve Kroft, Hillary was a far cry from the imposing figure we know today. Back then, her long blonde hair, fluffy bangs, and ubiquitous headband had many believing she was just another political wifey.

But she soon came out swinging, announcing she wouldn't be baking cookies; instead, she said she'd decided "to fulfill my profession which I entered before my husband was in public life." She pissed a large number of women off, but she also let us know how far her ambition would extend and that her husband would not be a limiting factor.

Which brings us to the present.

I want 2016 to be every bit as historic as 2008, but with a different "first" to celebrate. My daughters need Hillary in the Oval Office. Now 22 and 24, they're fully grown adults whose idealism has worn thin.

When Hillary formally announced her presidential campaign on April 12, 2015, I asked Jaye to sit down for a follow-up to her 2008 views on Hillary, politics, and sexism. Her answers were blunt, candid, and more cynical than I expected. Here's the transcript of our conversation:

What do you think of Hillary's candidacy?
"Good. We need women to run. If there were two candidates who were exactly the same, I'd vote for the woman."

Aren't you being sexist?
"This country needs a woman in a position of authority. A lot of people don't see that there's a glass ceiling. There are men that don't recognize what women struggle against. A female president would force those people to have respect for women.

"When you're young it's easy to imagine your future as a strong woman. You think you'll know how you'll behave if you face sexism, but once these things come into play there are a lot of gray areas. It's a lot more subtle: the supervisor who calls you sweetheart and would never say that to a man, the comments you overhear, the looks you get. There's never a single explosive incident, just a lot of small hits that take women down. It makes you realize that you are not on the same playing field.

"I didn't understand this in high school. Back then I saw men—teachers, mentors—as people who wanted to take care of you and had your best interests at heart. It's easy to be an idealist when you're young. But once you cross 16 and especially 18, men who once nurtured you now avoid you because they don't want to be seen as creepy. Other men with less integrity pretend to be your mentor, but they see you as a sexual object and that's why they're interested."

So how would a woman president change this?
"There are a lot of standards that presidents are held to. Because it's such a rigid environment, the protocols of how to interact with presidents would be the same regardless of gender; the protocol is respect. For a nation to respect

someone in terms of intelligence and leadership, the protocol would be that she's treated exactly like a man."

Do you feel as strongly about Hillary as you did when you were 16, 17?

"I would absolutely vote for her. I would like to volunteer for her campaign. I don't think I'll be as ridiculously gung-ho as I was in 2008. Back then I believed if I could shout it loud enough, I could convince others. I know the reality now; people have their minds set on who they'll vote for, and I can't change that. I also know that politics isn't appropriate in the workplace. I'd pin a Hillary button to my backpack or purse, but not on my clothing. In the workplace you want to be seen as neutral as possible, and I know my politics would impact my career."

It sounds like you've lost your idealism.

"I've gotten more pessimistic because I know how things actually work instead of how you think they'll work. Not everyone goes by the rules, and perfect systems don't exist.

"I still remember sitting in Chemistry class. I was excited, talking about Hillary Clinton, and that was when I realized I wasn't being supported, I was being made fun of. Someone parroted what I was saying in a mocking tone. It was a guy, and although he wasn't exactly mean, it made me aware."

But you vote.

"I think voting makes a difference, but I also believe the more well-informed I am, the more likely I am to be miserable. It's hard to see the injustices in the world and live with that knowledge. Ignorance really is bliss. I don't feel powerful enough to do anything about it. For a while, I followed Elizabeth Warren's campaign and was really excited about what she said, but then afterward I sank to a low point because I realized how little she can change things. Money screams louder than individual efforts."

Elizabeth Warren got to where she is on her own, but Hillary followed a path common to many female leaders—in the footsteps of a father or a spouse. Do you think that's why she's where she is today?

"When I think of Hillary, I don't even associate her with Bill. I think of him as the rock star president, but she's straightforward. There's nothing cool about her except that she's inherently awesome. But that's what's great. She works hard, and a lot of times when people elect someone, voters choose them because they want to have a beer with them. I don't want Hillary to be my friend or go shopping with me. I'm voting for her because I want her to lead the country."

At a time in our culture when so many women try to be their daughters' best friends and not their mothers, it's telling that Jaye doesn't want that from Hillary. If the role of a mother is to be responsible for—and firm with—her children, perhaps that explains why so many Great White Fathers have failed us. We don't need Dad's benevolence. We need Mom's tough love. That's why Hillary Clinton just might be the president this country needs to straighten up and fly right.

No More Glass Slippers
Kim Cottrell

If the shoe doesn't fit, must we change the foot?
—Gloria Steinem

Some people are obsessed with Hillary Clinton's hair, others with her pantsuits and what they say about her. They love to read about her fashion as if her style choices are tea leaves that can be divined to know her better. As for me? I fixate on her shoes and the lines on her face, along with her impressive accomplishments as a diplomat.

In my research of the Hillary obsessions of others, as well as my own, I Googled the phrase "Hillary Clinton feet." The search revealed a photo of her as secretary of state on a trip to France in 2010. In the picture, she ascended the steps at Élysée Palace in Paris toward a podium, and near the landing, her foot slipped out of her shoe. Then French President Nicolas Sarkozy helped her up the last steps and back into her shoe. That image made me wince a little. Who wouldn't wince and think of Cinderella at the ball tripping on her glass slipper while the coach and horsemen waited to whisk her away before midnight? As I viewed that image, I wondered why we "hobble" women with footwear.

Not only do we humans hobble livestock—somehow tying their feet together so they won't run away—but we have at times also shackled and fettered other humans to keep them from escaping. And there are times when we women even shackle ourselves. It's doubtful many of us think of ill-fitting shoes as a hobble or fetter, but Cinderella's glass slipper showed us otherwise, as did Secretary of State Hillary Clinton losing her shoe in Paris. Regardless of what we call it, nothing more effectively limits freedom than a rope or chain around ankles or an ill-fitting heel.

Women have shoe stories on both sides of the partisan divide. Democrat and former Speaker of the House Nancy Pelosi is known for her tasteful high heels that often match her suit color. There are reports about the shoes that make us feel powerful, like the military camouflage pumps worn by Republican Senator Joni Ernst, who is also an Iraq War veteran, to the 2015 State of the Union Address. There are tales of sling-backs that pinch so we slip them off and carry them. Or the platform heels that nearly cause us to break an ankle, and the mules that create blisters, or worse. And let's not forget the terribly expensive designer stilettos we can only stand in, as motionless as a trapped creature. In each case, women have put off important things while tending to their feet.

Despite the self-inflicted hobbling effect, women's high heels are so symbolic of perceived power they inspire some to pay for the surgical removal of a portion of the fourth metatarsal to fit into ever taller, pointier heels, as if taller and pointier represents even greater power. Yes, this surgery is a thing, as violent and hobbling as foot binding. Whether or not a woman undergoes this surgery, decades of wearing high-heels and other ill-fitting shoes deforms the foot and leaves the woman in pain.

But what if our ability to advance in business and politics was enhanced simply by fully supporting ourselves so we could easily stand upright without falling over? What if the glass slippers we wear so willingly prevent us from breaking through that last and highest glass ceiling—electing the first woman president of the United States? What if our most important resources are resilience, agility, and quickness of mind and body? It's worth pondering these questions because if ever there was an article of clothing that takes away women's actual power, including Hillary's, it's the hobble shoe.

Shoe designers are more than capable of creating fashionable and functional shoes for the on-the-go powerful woman. It might shock us how quickly attractive and comfortable shoes could flood the market, which really begs the question, why hobble shoes are still a thing after all these years? In 1910, one Mrs. Hart O. Berg matter-of-factly wrapped a rope around her knees to secure her skirt on a flight with Wilbur Wright, creating the short-lived fashion of the "hobble skirt." Just as the hobble skirt was rejected almost as quickly as it came on the scene about a century ago, maybe now is the time to say goodbye to the hobble shoe once and for all. The first female American president could matter-of-factly say goodbye to shoes that shackle.

Maybe our reluctance to ditch the hobble shoe reveals not only our perceptions of power, but also our sense of being ultra-feminine. While that's likely true for some, maybe others are waiting for a research study to prove unhobbled women are more collaborative, or more freethinking, or more healthy, or simply in less pain. But while we mull and mill around, waiting, maybe it's worth examining another Cinderella tale to understand how we might take matters into our own hands and live with greater power.

In a Slavic version of Cinderella called "Vasalisa," a young girl's mother is dying, but before she takes her last breath, she gives her daughter a tiny doll that resembles the girl. The mother instructs Vasalisa to keep the tiny doll in her pocket and give it food and water. She tells her to listen and follow the doll's instructions. After the mother dies and after a time of mourning, the father remarries. When the father goes away on a hunting trip, the new stepmother puts out the fire in their home and sends Vasalisa out into the forest to get fire from the old witch Baba Yaga, confident the girl won't survive. In the dark forest, Vasalisa consults the doll her mother gave her and correctly answers Baba Yaga's questions, and Baba Yaga gives her the fire. Vasalisa returns home, starts the fire in the hearth, and magically the stepmother and her daughters, who had hoped Vasilisa would be the one to disappear, are themselves gone by morning.

Without a script for welcoming a female presidential candidate, let alone a female presidential candidate with lines on her face, it's as if we citizens are the ones walking the dark path to Baba Yaga's hut. Along the way, demons will chase us and glimmers of faux-fire will lure us off the trail. Now, more than ever, we could benefit from consulting our doll-in-the-pocket intuition, retaining our focus and ignoring naysayers, and nimbly walking in beautiful, soft shoes rather than the fabled glass slippers Cinderella wore.

If we can work with the likes of Baba Yaga, the witch, to get the fire, we can work with ourselves to succeed in our quests. In the same way Baba Yaga might raise an eyebrow and grunt at a woman navigating the forest in Cinderella slippers, we can raise an internal eyebrow when we hobble our own actions. We can ask ourselves tough questions, like the ones Baba Yaga asked Vasalisa before deciding she was worthy of the gift of fire. Questions like, why should I help you? Vasalisa didn't apologize for what she was asking for or trip over herself to answer. Instead, she stood firmly and consulted the doll. Then, she calmly replied, "Because I asked," which left Baba Yaga to grudgingly nod and move on to the next question.

What if we took a moment to consult the doll we each carry in our pocket—you, Hillary and me? Can we get beyond old story lines and work together? Can we open the circle to women who've defended the fettered story? Can we resist the impulse to vent frustrations and opinions about how things went last time? Can we sweep the hearth free of the old debris and practice listening to our intuition, ignoring naysayers, and walking sure-footedly?

It shouldn't surprise us when Hillary, in the wisdom-wrinkled freedom she shares with most women over the age of fifty, remembers her own Cinderella glass slipper moment and chuckles at the past, firmly casting it aside. She knows being in control doesn't involve stooping down to delicately adjust a shoe while crossing the Capitol Rotunda or climbing steps to greet a head of state. No doubt, from now on Hillary will reserve the slippers that fetter for the ballroom. Perhaps, some of us will follow her lead and begin a trend toward more powerfully navigating our daily lives. Hillary knows, and we know, that the winner of this next presidential election will be the one solidly connected with the ground and with the electorate, the one nimble in movement and nimble in thought.

I can already guess how Hillary would behave as president, should she be nominated and then elected. I can guess because Hillary, as secretary of state, showed us exactly what to expect of Hillary as president. Hillary would do as any woman would do. In order to juggle the reading of copious reports, updating leaders and advisors, and preparing for the next meeting, she would put on her pantsuit of the day, pull back her hair, and slip into her sensible non-hobble shoes, ready to perform her duties, efficiently and without distraction.

So here's my idea, Hillary friends. Let's lace up our own shoes—you know the kind—tie back our hair, and celebrate the badass lines on our faces, the way our countrymen have been doing since forever, and get to work. If we are to retain our self-designated superpower status as a nation, we will do so when we unhobble women and unshackle men and let them go to work together creating a shared vision of the future—wrinkles, flaws, and all.

Six Degrees of Hillary Clinton: My Chappaqua Neighbor

Helen Jonsen

Election Day 2014 was the midterm election for the lame-duck years of President Barack Obama. Being self-employed, I avoided the crowds and waited until mid-morning to cast my ballot at our school polling place in Chappaqua, New York, often described as a leafy suburb an hour north of Grand Central Terminal. As I spoke to the volunteer to register, I heard the familiar voices of another voter or two who arrived next to me at the table. To my right were my neighbors, Hillary Rodham Clinton and President Bill Clinton. They, too, had come to meet their civic duty—to vote for our federal and state representatives, local judges, and governor.

We exchanged pleasantries and headed to the little kiosks to fill out our ballots. Secret Service men dressed as casually as the Clintons stood near them in the room. Little by little, others noticed them, but there was no press, no cameras. A number of people asked about their new granddaughter.

Outside, two black SUVs stood at the curb in the bus lane of the closed suburban school that serves as our polling place. When the Clintons came out alone, not in a hurry, I said hello again. They don't know me well but for fifteen years our paths have crossed both here in this berg and elsewhere. So we spoke for a while, not about politics but about mutual friends and acquaintances and local interests. Part of the conversation centered on how much they enjoy living in a town where their privacy has been reasonably protected and where they are comfortable dining, walking, shopping—even voting—without interruption (when reporters don't have a reason to stalk them, that is).

I have been a television and digital journalist for many years, so I always walk a fine line when it comes to running into the Clintons. I don't look for scoops but have sometimes been assigned to "cover" them. I am not *paparazza*. When not working, I've settled into the role of observer and neighbor, in their company when our paths cross. This has given me a glimpse into their lives and a perspective about them as people, rather than mere politicians, that others rarely get.

Fifteen years ago, when Hillary Clinton decided she would run for the U.S. Senate in New York, she went house hunting. Ironically, for me, it was the same summer my husband and I were looking for a new community for our family, complete with four children. It became something of a running gag that Hillary seemed to be following us. I would spend a day with a real estate agent in a Westchester town, and the next day the newspaper would report Hillary had been house hunting in the same community. Our price range was more than a million dollars apart from the former first couple, but we seemed to be looking in similar areas. Finally, I thought I had outrun them by moving to Chappaqua, a town a little further afield.

In 1999, Chappaqua was just another northern Westchester County "bedroom community" with a dichotomy—split between local families who had made their lives and businesses here for generations, and newer transplants that crowded the morning train platforms, ready for their hour-long commute to Grand Central Terminal. It's far enough away from New York City that the well-heeled and the well-known can live discreetly and quietly, yet make it into Manhattan relatively easily. At that point, the only notable long-ago resident with his name on buildings and streets was an early gentleman farmer, newspaper mogul, and one-time presidential candidate, Horace Greeley, known best for his famous quote, "Go West, young man." By the dawn of the new millennium, Greeley's memory had faded like the patina on the statue of him that welcomed drivers off the Saw Mill River Parkway. Newer celebrity names were bandied about, including actress and former Miss America Vanessa Williams, who had grown up in town, whose parents were teachers, and who chose to raise her own kids here.

To our surprise, that August weekend in 1999, as we unpacked a mountain of boxes in our new house, trying to find kitchen supplies, bedding, and kids' shoes, helicopters hovered above our heads. Unbeknownst to us, the day before, the Clintons came to meet the owners of the white Dutch colonial on nearby Old House Lane and closed their own deal on a new home. They walked across lawns and introduced themselves to a few of the neighbors—ironically they were the only ones we sort of knew before moving in. It was clear that sleepy Chappaqua would soon be on the GPS of every news desk in the nation and that Hillary and I were destined to share an adopted hometown. Not long after, the local Gannett newspaper headline read: "First Family of Chappaqua," along with five articles about the house, the deal, the hamlet, and how life might change for the citizenry because of the new neighbors.

Bill Clinton would be in the White House for more than a year after the purchase, but he and Hillary took possession of the charming colonial in November. In those first couple of months, fences were thrown up, security updated, and Secret Service moved into a rented Cape Cod up the hill from us, with access to the Clintons' home via the driveway and backyard of other friends. Black cars and men in dark suits with curly cords tucked behind their ears became common sights.

Sleepy Chappaqua would never be the same.

There were plenty of things to complain about having the Clintons as our neighbors. Folks who owned homes more expensive than the Clintons or who lived in town for many years were concerned with the anticipated disruption. Some criticized Hillary's perceived New York carpetbagging and the intrusion of the press in their quiet town. The state posted "No Parking" signs along the town's winding roads to keep gawkers at bay.

When motorcades drove out of the Clintons' dead-end street onto NY Route 117, one of my main travel roads, as well as a primary truck and school bus route, normally flowing traffic had no choice but to stop and wait. If the president wanted coffee at Starbucks, the village came to a standstill until his caravan sped away heading for Manhattan or Westchester Airport. ("Doesn't he have a coffee maker?" asked one friend.) Our town bristled at the added cost of police overtime for Clinton escort and surveillance. But it wasn't just the traffic issues that initially irritated town residents. Everyone remembered Hillary's infamous comment about not "staying home" and "making cookies," again insulting area professional women who gave up jobs to raise their kids and other working moms who were doing both. And, not surprisingly, there were titters about "locking up our daughters" and hoping "no interns" would be at the house.

But when spring of 2000 came and her U.S. Senate campaign was well underway, First Lady Hillary surprised us with her desire to actually be a part of our community. We were delighted when she asked the Girl Scouts if she could march with them in our town Memorial Day parade.

Just when we thought things might calm down as President Clinton came to the end of his presidency, on his last day in office, he became embroiled in a pardon controversy. The press swooped in as never before. Live TV trucks parked in front of our supermarket and train station. Camera crews staked out the cul-de-sac in front of their gated and Secret Service-protected driveway. It was the month the Clintons planned to leave the

White House, so we expected some end-of-term Clinton traffic, as Bill was returning to Chappaqua full-time with plans to write his memoirs, but nothing like the onslaught we experienced. Hillary, however, bought a house in Georgetown as her Washington residence, plotting her own place on Capitol Hill.

By March, with the pardon scandal losing news traction but still of interest, only one TV "pool news" crew remained behind the cul-de-sac barricade to keep tabs on the now-former president. March was also Girl Scout cookie time in Chappaqua. My oldest daughter, a fifth-grade Junior Girl Scout, sold cookies door-to-door through the neighborhood one weekend, including Old House Lane and the Clinton house where we approached the Secret Service booth. The Fox News media pool crew was on high alert when anyone approached the Clinton home. After a phone call or two from booth to house, President Clinton came through the gate with his Labrador, Buddy, and paused for my daughter to ask if he would like to buy cookies. "I'll take two," he said as he watched her write his name on the official Girl Scout form. "What kind would you like?" she asked as she showed him the photos. "The plain kind," he said in his southern drawl, meaning the classic shortbread Trefoils.

My children and I could have been selling cookies to any neighbor on any street, but here were my children talking to our former president as if he were any other neighbor. The footage of my kids and Bill Clinton would air on the national news that night and would also surface later in the year when pundits speculated on whether the Clintons were living together or apart. Neighbors sometimes wondered the same. But later that year, in the wake of the terrorist attacks on September 11, the Clintons showed up together at a synagogue for an interfaith service organized by the local churches and temples. They attended, not to speak, but to observe and, perhaps, pray—again, to be part of their new community.

After Hillary took her Senate seat on Capitol Hill, she was

something of a weekender. I didn't see our hometown pal as much. Local police noted that Senator Clinton would often fly in and out of the county airport, fifteen minutes from her house, on Friday nights and head to other parts of the state on Saturday mornings to make the rounds with her constituents. Meanwhile, Bill was holed up here with his writing and could be seen any day taking a walk around town like a Chappaqua regular.

Hillary continued to find ways to truly become part of our community. She soon added our annual Community Day to her schedule in September 2002, a Saturday afternoon each autumn where every organization and business in our town hosts a booth to meet and mingle with town residents. Hillary walked from stall to stall, posed for pictures, and hung out for a while with my troop and me at the Girl Scouts booth. She was clearly making a concerted effort to embrace her new, mostly Democratic liberal hometown in a way that resonated with Chappaqua residents and the rest of New York's voters.

As the years have passed, despite their travels and a home in D.C., Bill and Hill have become regulars in many of our shops and restaurants—haircuts, deli runs, coffee in Starbucks, buying gifts, or getting the dogs groomed. Photos with them and shop owners hang proudly on almost every wall in Chappaqua and surrounding towns. The Clintons could just as easily hide. But they don't. When she was senator and folks were surprised to see her pushing a cart at the supermarket, Hillary quipped later, "I have to eat, too!"

In what seemed like a gift from any local author, Bill Clinton held book signings for his memoir in 2004, and his second book in 2011. Crowds stood in line for hours. Hillary followed suit with *Hard Choices* in June 2014. Hundreds lined up at our library to exchange a word and a laugh. In return, after the September birth of Chelsea's baby, the volunteers at the Chappaqua Children's Book Festival sent a basket of books to baby Charlotte, in care of grandma's house.

Hillary has either been running for something or serving in some public office during most of her time in Chappaqua. She has been First Lady, U.S. senator, presidential candidate, secretary of state, devoted daughter, author, mother, grandmother, private citizen, and ... now presidential candidate again. But I think she left the carpetbagger label behind once she became a local mother-of-the-bride. The then Secretary of State Hillary told *Working Mother* magazine president and another Chappaqua mom, Carol Evans, that her mobile phone allowed her to help Chelsea make wedding plans from wherever she was in the world. Even though Hillary could have ordered any wedding item from anywhere in the world, she chose a local pastry shop to make her daughter's wedding cake, a decision that surely made town residents proud.

But the town's Memorial Day Parade has become her most visible day in town. Hillary has marched every year since that first time with the Girl Scouts. Often with the former president, she attends the wreath-laying tributes and takes her place at the lead with other elected officials. Time permitting, she has remained for the memorial ceremonies honoring the town's war dead, and, of course, posing for countless pictures. She once told *The New York Times*, "I put this on my calendar every year, and I basically tell my staff I really, really, really want to do this." Even as secretary of state, she said, "So unless there's some crisis of significant proportion, I'll be here, and I've had a few crises where I've had to take phone calls as I've marched."

And she's made sure to be aware of difficult times in our community. In 2014, she presented a plaque to the local dry cleaners' family whose son was killed in Afghanistan. It was a moving moment for all of us.

The Clintons have even established a Christmas Eve tradition in our hamlet. Bill and Hill personally (sometimes one or both) go through town giving gifts to the businesses they frequent and wishing them "Merry Christmas." Then they dine at Crabtree's

Kittle House and Restaurant for Christmas Eve dinner, along with a packed restaurant. It's one of their go-to spots year-round. Sometimes they dine there with Chelsea, friends, or supporters. They often host their holiday staff parties there, and join in the Fourth of July barbecue. It was the venue for Chelsea's baby shower (with no paparazzi in sight) and, in one news report, owner John Crabtree listed a few of the world leaders who have dined there with them (with no press around): former German Chancellor Helmut Kohl, former Israeli Prime Minister Ehud Barak, and Rwanda's President Paul Kagame.

Rumors swirled a few years ago that the one-time first couple might move out of Chappaqua, buying a multimillion dollar grander estate in a horsey celebrity-ridden town a few miles north. But it didn't happen. Hillary has updated the interior of the house and told a local magazine she enjoys entertaining there, so it certainly seems as though they are here to stay ... unless there is an upcoming detour to the White House.

While the national press called First Lady Hillary stiff and unyielding, cold in some ways, we in Chappaqua witnessed the thaw that happened early on. Here, she became an open neighbor who found time to contribute to the community, took part in events, and spoke to school groups. As someone who is still our neighbor, we see the human side, the easy laugh and genuine interest in whatever conversation she is holding. We see her long-term commitments in life played out just by staying put. As neighbors, it's become a pleasure to have the Clintons in the roles of just plain folks—that human and humane softer image Hillary's campaign has always hoped to capture but hasn't. Ask us. It's there.

When the Clintons and I spoke outside the elementary school on that Election Day, I didn't get any insights into Hillary's political future or if she had at that point decided whether she was going to take another run at the presidency. In that moment, though, I had the feeling she was in no hurry to leave our hometown, where she and Bill will celebrate their fortieth wedding anniversary.

Whether I choose to vote for Hillary Rodham Clinton this time around, we will once again cast our ballots in the same room in our adopted hometowns, a school cafeteria where my daughters attended school. Together we share in a small piece of history already: voting where the first First Lady in history to run for president finds her name on the ballot, casting a vote in our shared adopted hometown.

Bill Clinton as Metaphor for America and Why Hillary Is Uniquely Qualified for President

Rebekah Kuschmider

"*Why does she stay with him?*"

I remember that question from 1998. President Bill Clinton had had an affair with a White House intern, and women—at least women I knew—were collectively outraged on behalf of the First Lady. This wasn't his first rumored affair, and Hillary Clinton was a feminist, right? She was a lawyer who could make her own way. No one would fault her for walking away. Why would she stay?

Why *would* she stay? Maybe the question we should have asked is this: why was Hillary with Bill in the first place?

Remember the Bill Clinton of 1992? He was the slow-talking Southern charmer, playing the saxophone on *The Arsenio Hall Show* and talking about his underwear on MTV. He was handsome and so smart, a Rhodes Scholar even. He sauntered through the campaign, unseated poor George H.W. Bush, put his cocky, appealing feet up on the desk in the Oval Office, and declared himself in charge.

Then he spent the next three years pissing off Congress. He installed his wife Hillary on a commission to fix the health care industry, he started making noise about equality for gay people, and he swore to fix Social Security first. But "Hillary Care" failed and gay people were instructed to not ask or tell, while Bill signed the Defense of Marriage Act into law and Social Security is still broken, all these years later.

Then Bill's second term was all Monica Lewinsky, all the time, and we all watched Republicans throw good money after bad investigating Bill's investments (can you say "Whitewater"), his relationships, and everything else they could think of. Al Gore ran away from him on the campaign trail and so did the Supreme Court; when all the dust settled, they declared the Clinton years done and over in 2000.

Oh, Bill. So much promise. So many flaws. So brilliant. So riddled with hubris. Bill, the American Icarus sailing so very high and falling in a heap. Then, from an office in Harlem, Icarus turned Phoenix and rose from the ashes and began soaring around the world, bringing that old Bill magic to impoverished places with a goal to make the world a better place. And damned if he doesn't seem to be doing it, and don't we all love him again? Don't we see him on late-night talk shows or in Chelsea's maternity ward room or on stage at the Democratic National Convention and settle in for the good stuff we know is coming? We do. We love Bill.

But I think Hillary must love Bill the most.

In her memoir *Living History*, she called Bill a force of nature and she resisted his marriage proposals for a long time because she didn't know if she could weather his storms. But once she said yes, she made that yes matter. Hillary stood by her brilliant, imperfect husband when the rest of us would have walked away. She weathered his storms and continues to weather them. She appeared deaf to the criticism of his character, his morals, his ethics. She never said a harsh word against him. They seem to walk in lockstep, regardless of circumstances, these two living American icons, loyal to one another year after year, victory after victory, catastrophe after catastrophe.

For years people have wondered about the substance of their marriage and what it all means that Hillary stayed. Is it love or sex or coattails or politics or money or Chelsea or what is it? What keeps them together? Why this unwavering loyalty? Through thick and thin: loyal. Rich or poor: loyal. Powerful or disgraced: loyal. Sick or well: loyal. Whatever else you can say about the Clintons, and there is so much, you have to admit that they are loyal to each other.

In 1998, we saw that loyalty as a blind and foolish thing, a woman standing by her man, even though she'd claimed years before that she would never be like a Tammy Wynette, when her man didn't stand by her. It looked like weakness back then or maybe a betrayal of a certain kind of ideal—wifeliness over feminism. Now, though, I wonder. Is that loyalty, that devotion to a union, possibly Hillary's greatest strength?

There has never been a day in the history of America that the promise of the idea wasn't shadowed by the missteps of the people. As the Founding Fathers trumpeted a hard-fought freedom, slaves toiled in the fields, dying as they built the nation that called them five-eighths of a human. When the Industrial Revolution came and transformed the economy and global trade, women took to machines in factories like the Triangle Shirtwaist firetrap, where they worked for lower wages than a man would get, even as they were denied the vote that might have allowed them to ask Congress and the president for worker protections. When Johnny marched to Europe to fight the Axis powers, Navajo soldiers lent their lives and their language to the war effort of a nation that systematically tried to exterminate their forebears. When the Space Age rocketed forth and America beat Russia to the moon, a young girl named Hillary Rodham wrote to NASA asking how to become an astronaut only to be told they "weren't interested" in women.

We are still working out all the ways that the American people, immigrant and indigenous, man and woman, black and white, gay and straight, can work together to live up to the dream of a place that's supposed to be of the people, by the people, and for the people. We all look back at history and vow to redeem ourselves of the sins of our fathers, or to forgive the descendants of those who sinned against our fathers. We find a way to love this imperfect place, generation after generation.

When America betrayed Hillary's dream of going to space, she forgave and found another way to serve, another way to soar. When America turned on her husband and chased through their closet tossing skeletons into the light, she forgave and stayed loyal to the man and the office he held. When America turned down her offer to be our president in 2008, she forgave the man we chose instead and served him as his chief diplomat for five years, representing America across the globe and offering its strength and promise to a world that might not see the good among the bad.

Hillary loves Bill, yes. Hillary loves the real Bill, good and bad, weak and strong, right and wrong. But maybe Hillary loves America more, the real America, good and bad, weak and strong, right and wrong. That love, that loyalty, that ability to see the real America—the raw, striving, gasping with hope America—is Hillary's strength, a nearly wifely attitude of loyalty—in richer and poorer, sickness and health, weakness and strength. A steadfast determination to stay, despite everything, and make it work with America, to stay and make it work with us, the way she's always stayed and made it work with Bill.

All of that is what makes Hillary special. It even makes her—dare I say it—presidential.

I Walk the Line:
Hillary Clinton vs. Elizabeth Warren
Aliza Worthington

John F. Kerry wrote a poignant forward to the 2014 book about the iconic 1960's folk group, Peter, Paul and Mary. Yes, THAT John F. Kerry—the man who took over as secretary of state after Hillary Clinton's departure, and former U.S. senator from Massachusetts. In the foreword, he writes with great poetry and beauty about the impact the folk group had on him throughout formative and tumultuous times in his life, and of his eventual friendship with and inspiration from members of the group. Of Mary, he wrote:

> . . . she was always guided by advice she got from her mother: "Be careful of compromise," she said. "There's a very thin line between compromise and accomplice."

Walking that thin line feels like every presidential election in which I've participated. Voting, for me, has always been done with an eye more toward realism than idealism—balancing what rang right and true for me with my reservations. Barack Obama got my vote in both national elections, but in the 2008 primaries, I was extremely torn between him and Hillary Clinton. When she lost the Democratic presidential nomination, I eagerly got behind Obama, happily allowing my idealism to take over. This involved putting aside my qualms over his inexperience compared to hers and letting my ally flag fly high and proud, crying tears of joy at his inauguration. I don't begin to regret either of my votes for him.

So what do Mary's words have to do with Hillary Clinton and how I feel about her as my potential future president? Well, in choosing whose candidacy to support in 2016, it crystalized the discomfort I feel in supporting her. No one can argue with a straight face that she isn't spectacularly qualified. Yet, she's made decisions and formed ties about which I'm deeply conflicted, and therein lies the rub.

Her ties to big money make me squeamish, and I'm not a fan of her early support of the war in Iraq. With the benefit of time (and impetus of presidential ambition, I'm sure), Hillary has distanced herself from those things, voicing regrets about them. Take, for example, a certain Congressional vote that would have ended up hurting the poor and working class. She voted for the 2001 Bankruptcy bill, making renegotiating credit card debt harder while making it easier for the wealthy to protect their assets. It died, but a similar version was passed in 2005 (Clinton missed the 2005 vote but says she would have opposed it.). She plainly says she "got it wrong" in her vote for the Iraq War, as well. I can accept whatever combination of hindsight, wisdom, and political expediency motivated her to shift toward this direction I prefer. Perhaps, cynically, I felt Clinton was the best the Democrats could do.

Until Elizabeth Warren. Oh, Elizabeth, how you seem like the perfect antidote to virtually all societal ills—and perhaps you are! You bring such passion and intelligence to championing the poor and putting Wall Street *In. Its. Place.* that it's hard to want anybody else to be the Democratic standard bearer in 2016. Talk about feeling like I'm compromising.

Yet another part of me wants, more than anything, for Elizabeth Warren to remain exactly where she is, in the U.S.

Senate, kicking *ASS* on the Committee on Banking, Housing & Urban Affairs and taking *NAMES* on the Committee on Health, Education, Labor & Pensions.

I'm fully aware that the president has the national bully pulpit, can set agendas, send proposed legislation to Congress, and sign legislation into law when it arrives on his or her desk. This is no small matter. The president of the United States operates from a position of tremendous strength in many ways.

Congress, though, is where the legislation is created and passed. That's where decisions about money are MADE. It is where arguments are hashed out, funds are allocated, and where my gut feels like Senator Warren can make the greatest difference in the lives of the greatest number of ordinary Americans. With Republicans in control of both Houses of Congress, I want Elizabeth Warren there to hold their feet to the fire. I want her there to expose the inevitable bullshit being thrown around as legislation struggles to be formed. I want her there to call out centrist Democrats who, make no mistake, indulge in and benefit from the same cronyism and self-serving motives so many Republicans do. That's where I want Senator Elizabeth Warren.

While this may sound contradictory, I would be thrilled to see Warren RUN for the White House. I'm not the only one who feels that the entire Democratic Party benefits when there is more than one serious competitor for a party nomination. U.S. Senator Bernie Sanders of Vermont and former Maryland Governor Martin O'Malley are already in the running. But if Warren jumped in, as well, they would all push Hillary to seriously address the things about which so many of us are uncomfortable, like her relationship with Wall Street, her Iraq War vote, and her support of welfare reform. I'm in favor of pushing Clinton more to the left, getting her to articulate a more progressive agenda than she might if left alone in the field with her comfortable connections to Wall Street.

Having a strong and diverse field from which to choose a

nominee enhances, rather than detracts from, the eventual front-runner. As the editors of *The Nation* explained beautifully:

> [This] is about whether the party will speak to the real
> concerns of voters. We need a Democratic presidential
> candidate with a smart, populist program untethered to
> Wall Street and committed to dismantling a rigged system
> that enriches the very few at the expense of everyone else.

It sounds a lot like *The Nation* would prefer a Warren or Sanders nomination, and while in an ideal world, I might like that, too, I'm opting for realism in supporting Hillary.

Where does that fall on my Mary Travers scale? Is that compromise? Is it accomplice? A deeper look into Hillary's long, complex political history may help me decide.

Some say the baggage she carries will weigh her down, but there are also signs the electorate has matured enough to check those bags at the curb. In a Pew Research Center poll published in March 2014, only 17 percent of respondents thought Hillary's "involvement" with Bill Clinton's administration would hurt her, and only 20 percent felt the fact that she's a woman would be a detriment. Forty-four percent felt her gender wouldn't make a difference—an increase of eight percent over the same poll question in 2008.

But what about the "B" word so often unfairly associated with Hillary? No, not "bitch." No, not "bossy." That's right. "Benghazi." In November 2014, a Republican-controlled House committee put to rest (although I'm sure they will come up again) allegations that Hillary botched her response to the attack on our embassy in Benghazi while she was secretary of state that resulted in the deaths of four Americans, including our ambassador to Libya, J. Christopher Stevens. The investigation took two years and determined there was ". . . no intelligence failure, no delay in sending a CIA rescue team, no missed opportunity for a military rescue . . . " So sayeth a committee whose majority was REPUBLICAN.

As for Hillary's accomplishments, they stand on their own. Even the conservative *Wall Street Journal* wrote, "[s]he can position herself as an antidote to Washington dysfunction, playing up her experience as a former senator and top diplomat who knows how to reach consensus." Hillary's record as a champion for health care, her work on behalf of the Children's Defense Fund, and her senatorial reputation for bipartisanship are well known and well documented.

She has spent a good deal of energy as secretary of state impressing upon other world leaders the importance of quality education for women, along with equal pay and fair treatment for women around the world. She plainly and forcefully advocates for clean water, healthy food, and access to health care for women and children around the globe. Specifically, Hillary launched the "Saving Mothers, Giving Life" initiative, which aims to reduce maternal and neonatal deaths by 50 percent. Its website reports that the maternal mortality rate has declined by 30 percent in Uganda and 35 percent in Zambia, with an impressive increase of women giving birth in health facilities in both countries—all in the first year of the program.

During Hillary's tenure as secretary of state, the State Department developed a website called www.slaveryfootprint. org. This poignantly artistic site helps people understand, and work to break, their everyday connection to what is the equivalent of modern-day slavery—in other countries, and our own.

Global Post, an online news site, has rightly characterized gender equality and women and children's health as among Hillary's "core areas of interest, which have been central to her approach to foreign policy, health, development, and security."

So looking at her through this multi-faceted lens, I ask myself if support for Hillary as president of the United States is compromise or accomplice. The answer is neither. It isn't compromise to elect someone imperfect. In fact, it is a guarantee. The question I ask myself is, which candidate has imperfections I can tolerate best, when viewing the candidate as a whole?

The notion that the advancement of a society is directly proportional to the status of its women has been often expressed in one form or another over the centuries. Given that our domestic and global cultures have a long way to go on this front, and given the fact that the status of women influences everything from economic conditions to foreign policy, supporting Hillary Clinton, even with reservations, starts to feel better than simply compromising.

To me, it feels right.

Embracing the Parents' Agenda for the Win

KJ Dell'Antonia

For all the talk of winning over "soccer moms" and "boomer grandmas" and even "NASCAR dads," families historically don't vote as a bloc. In the coming presidential election, that could change. Hillary Clinton needs families, and, with the right agenda in 2016, she could be the candidate to win them over.

Hillary Clinton has long voiced her passionate advocacy for a variety of family issues, from her book *It Takes a Village* to the Clinton Foundation's "Too Small to Fail" campaign. But she's done relatively little—yet—to promote policies that back up those words by offering real support to families in the form of paid sick leave, paid family leave, and better access to child care and early education programs. Now is her chance, and taking advantage of it could prove to be a win-win for both candidate and voters.

Parents need policies that support them in supporting their families, and Hillary Clinton—who wasn't always a First Lady, senator, or secretary of state with a staff on call—knows it. She has described being summoned to court in her working lawyer days when her babysitter called in sick and Bill Clinton was out of town (a friend stepped in to help with then-two-year-old Chelsea). She has gone home to a demanding child after a long day and a long commute. More recently, she canceled an overseas trip as secretary of state to rush to her elderly mother's hospital bed. She knows what it's like for many of us as we try to manage work and family.

Those experiences set her apart from a long line of presidential candidates both Democrat and Republican, who have people around them to insulate them from that daily struggle—in a word, wives. In her 2008 presidential campaign, Hillary was burned many times by her attempts to be honest about her experience as a working parent (witness the backlash from the faux "cookies" controversy of 1992), leading her to largely sidestep her groundbreaking status as the first woman with a real shot at the office by running instead on health care and foreign policy. In 2016, she could embrace the obvious and use her personal history to grab the agenda that President Barack Obama set in his 2015 State of the Union address—paid family and sick leave, universal preschool, and an expanded earned-income tax credit and child tax credit—and run both with and on it.

Just as Hillary is far more than a "woman's candidate," family is far more than a "women's issue"; but if that's the label that's likely to be applied, then it's in her best interest to grab the chance to make a family agenda her own. If she does, she'll put family issues at the center of an election cycle that has yet to find a central defining debate—and that would be a great thing for all of us.

For years, the United States has been criticized for its status as an extreme world outlier in its support for families. After Australia passed its parental leave law in 2010, we became the only industrialized nation not to offer paid maternity leave. That failing has contributed to the United States being condemned for human rights violations by Human Rights Watch and ranked last in breastfeeding support by Save the Children. The case for national paid family leave has been brought up by everyone from feminist academics to Fox News anchors. An election centered on working to change that shameful status would be likely to benefit all families, no matter which side wins. In 2012, 36 percent of the electorate had children under the age of eighteen at home. The already Democratic-leaning young voters who first helped elect Obama in 2008 are now entering prime childbearing years, making the pro-family agenda of particular importance to a Democratic candidate, but large numbers of voters of every ilk stand to benefit from policies that support families. Most of us will be breadwinners and caregivers at some point in our lives. We have jobs and we have children, parents, and siblings who need us. Few of us can afford to have someone else on call to handle the moment when your father gives his nursing home attendant the slip or Bobby barfs all over math class, and, as Hillary knows, you don't send a staffer to your mother's final moments. Some of us are lucky enough to have the kinds of jobs that let us flex our hours to step up for emergencies and more. Most of us aren't. We all know how badly we need that flexibility. We need jobs that are still there when the crisis is over, and policies that help us get through the tough times we'll all face.

But family voters, like all voters, get distracted. We lose sight of the way programs like public preschool, subsidized day care, paid family leave, pregnancy discrimination protections, and paid sick days would help us, our neighbors, our children, and our parents both directly and indirectly. We get caught up in our national short-term fears rather than focusing on our long-term goals.

A straight-talking Hillary, like the one who tweeted, "The earth is round, the sky is blue, and #vaccineswork," could keep these issues front and center for all the candidates. She's a facts and figures kind of speaker with a mastery of anecdotes, who knows that one reason it's hard to balance the needs of work and family is that when we allow that balance to be set by market forces, family is on the losing side. Only 12 percent of us have access to paid family leave through our employers, and fewer than 40 percent more through short-term disability insurance. Hillary has long acknowledged that the unpaid leave promised by the federal Family and Medical Leave Act signed by her husband in 1993 doesn't go far enough. It only applies to less than 50 percent of workers, and many of those can't afford to take it. We can't even take leave to care for ourselves when we're sidelined with an illness: forty million workers in the U.S. don't have a single paid sick day.

With the current movement by other Democrats in the direction of an agenda meant to appeal to parents, Hillary Clinton has an opportunity to get voters fired up to change all that—and possibly to sweep her into office in the process. Family-friendly policies have deep middle-class appeal and would let her campaign on a message of expanding opportunity for working-age Americans. When questioned about cost, she can offer more facts and figures, like the numbers showing that while paid sick leave may cost businesses a little, it doesn't cost them much. In San Francisco, just one in seven businesses says it hurt their profits. In Connecticut, business-reported cost increases ranged from small to none. Both reported that price increases and cuts in hours or hiring were small.

Hillary could push for programs designed to fund themselves, like the Family and Medical Insurance Leave Act, a Social Security-style plan proposed by Senator Kirsten Gillibrand of New York and Representative Rosa DeLauro of Connecticut, that would provide all American workers with up to twelve weeks of partial income when they take time to care for themselves or a family member or for the birth or adoption of a child, paid for by small employee and employer payroll contributions of two-tenths of one percent of wages each (two cents per $10 in wages), or about $1.50 per week for a typical worker. In doing so, she could force the Republicans to find a family-friendly agenda of their own.

But this is an essay about Hillary, so let's imagine how she—almost certain to be the only woman on the general election stage—could run a "Put Families First" campaign. Over and over and over again, at every stop on the trail, Hillary could tell voters that while paid family and medical leave sound expensive, what's really costly is the endless merry-go-round of low-wage workers taking and leaving jobs as circumstances require them to take more time to care for their families than their jobs allow. Businesses who want to treat employees fairly, she could explain, are caught in a competitive trap: if all companies aren't held to the same standard, the need to keep costs down pulls the business standard down with it. At its extreme, that pressure leads to child labor and to locked doors in garment factories. Those things are a regrettable part of our national history; as a former secretary of state, Hillary Clinton knows that in some developing markets around the world, they're still a reality. She could tell a powerful story about why democracy and capitalism must intersect to give us the freedom to produce without the need to disregard basic human dignity.

Here at home, Hillary Clinton could remind all of us that low, low prices at the big box stores come at the cost of employees unable to care for themselves and their families. Our "savings" from failing to support those families represents a false economy. We bear the costs in different ways: in funding emergency rooms, providing public assistance even for full-time workers whose wages can't support their families, and in expensive incarceration for teenagers and young adults tempted by the greater income offered by drug sales or by the temporary releases of the drugs themselves.

And, after she has laid out the facts and figures, with her practical groundwork so clear, Hillary Clinton could get mad. Because there is so very much to be angry about, and she is perfectly poised to channel that rage.

Hillary Clinton can stride onto any platform, her daughter—

and her granddaughter—beside her, and talk about the needs of working women as well as the needs of working families in a way no male candidate ever has or, at least in this era, can, and in a way no woman has yet dared to do. No one can question her commitment to her career or to her family; she has bypassed the questioning that dogs so many female politicians about how they will balance work and family by launching her political career later in life. With an adult daughter, she has no need to avoid addressing the challenges of women with young children for fear that those will be seen as her challenges; she can tackle them head-on with her own personal stories, and with her hopes for future generations of women.

Imagine her declaring these words (adapted slightly from the "Too Small to Fail" website):

> *Budgets reflect choices. The way we spend our money is not just about economics; it's about our values and priorities. And we, as Americans, have made a disturbing choice.*
>
> *We have chosen not to support our families.*
>
> *We talk a good game, but at the federal and state levels, we have systematically chosen to invest in support for seniors, the military, "too big to fail" institutions, prisons—but we have consistently chosen not to protect and support children and their families.*

Imagine her, at her best, pounding the podium when she responds to the inevitable questions about how employers could afford to offer such fulsome benefits as a bare minimum of paid time to recover from the arrival of a child, or a week off to tend to a hospitalized parent, with a demand to know how we can afford not to. She could roar out all of our collective fury that a woman can lose her job over her inability to lift heavy packages during her pregnancy while a man with the same limitation as a result of a fall during a bar room brawl must be reassigned—because pregnancy is not a disability, but a slipped disc is, no matter the cause.

She could call on voters to rise up and demand the kind of early childhood education and child care that lets parents work to support their families and helps those children to someday grow up to be the breadwinners for their own families. Freed of years of holding back on these issues, she could demand that our nation find a way to lift up families to do the other work we need them to do: raising our future doctors, our future inventors, our future employees, and our future CEOS—and our future parents. Our country needs families, and families need us—and Hillary Clinton, flaunting her status as once-working mother and now proud grandmother, could be the right candidate to step up and say so. There haven't been very many moments in her political life when those things worked in her favor. There aren't very many moments when those things work in *any* woman's favor. It would be nice to see a politician make them work for us all.

Inspecting Hillary's Privilege Knapsack
Veronica I. Arreola

I f Hillary Rodham Clinton is to successfully shatter the now-infamous glass ceiling for women presidential candidates, she will need to grab a sledgehammer from her "privilege knapsack." Oh yes, that proverbial knapsack that Peggy McIntosh, former Associate Director of the Wellesley Centers for Women, taught so many of us about in 1989. That knapsack that holds so many of our unconsidered privileges, such as white privilege and class privilege, that color our perceptions. Hillary's bag holds the mighty sledgehammer that she requires to smash her way into the White House in her own right, and get the votes of women who don't carry that same knapsack, by taking a swing to break down some inherent problems in her well-intentioned family policies.

While Hillary and her entourage of consultants may think that the key to a 2016 White House victory is reestablishing the Democratic Party with white men, I contend that for her to succeed, she must win the hearts of low-income women and women of color. In 2008, President Barack Obama not only overwhelmingly won over African-American (95%), Latino (67%), and Asian (62%) voters, but he also triumphed with the majority of voters who earned less than $50,000 a year. He increased the edge with voters of color in 2012 and maintained favorability with low-income voters. According to The Brookings Institution and the Pew Research Center, the diversification of the electorate will only continue to grow, which suggests that any presidential candidate in the future must appeal to many diverse constituencies. As a Latina, I know that in order for Hillary to win us over, she needs to spend some quiet time with her privilege knapsack and show voters in those groups more respect. Sadly, she doesn't have a great record of doing that.

Don't get me wrong—I admire Hillary. I was born in her hometown of Park Ridge, Illinois. We both grew up root-root-rooting for the Chicago Cubs. We both centered our careers on the empowerment of girls and women. But I learned that empowerment is a complicated thing. While I was working on my master's degree, one of my professors announced that he had a list of words he refused to see in any of our research papers. "Empowered" was one of them. His rationale was eye-opening, even if it took me a while to truly "get it."

"Professor Empowered" claimed that no one could empower another person because people have their own power inside of themselves. Now, we could work in a manner that helped them see and use that power, but we could not give them power or empower anyone with anything they did not already have. At the time of his class, I was just beginning my career working to advance women in science and engineering. The very heart of my work was to empower girls and women to go into the sciences and flourish. When Professor E prohibited the word "empower," I felt as if he'd stolen a key term from my professional vocabulary. I recall nights trying to write paper after paper for him without using the word "empower." Years later, I realized that instead of looking for a synonym for that "e" word, I needed to readjust my frame of reference. Instead of thinking that I needed to "save women" from their lot in life, I had to stop to listen to their needs and learn from them how I could best support their work. Similarly, Hillary must readjust her frame of reference in 2016 if she wants to win our hearts, votes, and the White House.

In the summer of 2013, I attended the annual Clinton Global Initiative conference in Chicago. I was eager to hear Hillary speak in person. I was hoping to pick up on hints to a 2016 run at the White House and perhaps get a peek at how she'd position herself for a presidential bid. Would she embrace the woman-candidate label that she seemed to run from in 2008? Instead, I witnessed her reestablish her status as the empowering candidate. She exhibited little understanding of the struggles that low-income women and women of color—those she was seeking to "empower"—endure.

Hillary's speech that day about the need to educate girls and women around the world as the solution to global poverty struck the crowd as common sense. We clapped as she rattled off idea after idea. How difficult is it to suggest that simple basic education of girls is a good thing? How could we ignore the economic and health benefits of educating girls? All of her ideas seemed so easy, so obvious.

Then she got to the health of pregnant women and newborns, and said, "How do we make sure that pregnant women, particularly poor women, understand the nutrients they should take to support their own and their baby's health?"

And that got under my skin as thoughts of Professor Empowerment came back to me. On the surface, it seemed like an innocuous and non-controversial statement. But that's the privilege talking. My issue with her quote, and any future ones like it, is that it assumes ignorance as the reason for the lack of healthy prenatal care and subsequent issues with newborns. If she wants to win the support of lower-income women, I would ask Hillary to look past this first layer of "Why?" and dig deeper into the larger issue.

For example, for those of us with certain privilege, having a family doctor and being able to make medical appointments for ourselves and our kids is a given. But for many Americans, that's not the case, and Hillary knows that. The obstacles low-income women have in even obtaining prenatal care were a central theme to her 1994 pursuit of universal health care, and they have not gone away, even under Obamacare. Hillary knows full well that the first hurdle for many families is finding a provider who will see you when you have no insurance. And since Obamacare can still be difficult to get depending on where you live, that's not a blanket solution. But if you can even get access to a doctor, the next obstacle is finding the time to see a provider on your work schedule. Hillary once served on the board of Walmart, so she should know all too well that in most working-class jobs, one's schedule is not always known well enough ahead of time to plan a prenatal visit, much less handle well-baby or sick visits. According to *The New York Times*, San Francisco and Vermont have already moved to help part-time workers obtain schedules that allow for planning things such as well-baby visits. President Obama's call in early 2015 for seven paid sick days for all workers is a start. Hillary needs to push that as far as it can go.

I am ready for Hillary to tackle schedule flexibility.

I am ready for Hillary to tackle paid sick days.

Hillary also needs to dig around in her political knapsack when it comes to talking about nutrition in low-income communities. A vital part of good prenatal care is a healthy diet full of fresh vegetables and fruit. Hillary surely knows of the lack of access low-income people have to fresh and healthy food not only in our nation's big cities, but also in our rural communities. Yes, some of the people who help to feed our country and the world lack access to that same food. Food deserts are not solely an issue for big city mayors, but also for vast regions of the American heartland. Not eating well while pregnant is not simply an issue that can be solved with a brochure or public service announcement during daytime television, but one that requires thoughtful cooperation among fast-food restaurants, grocery stores, and the U.S. government.

And then there are the families who do have access to grocery stores that sell fresh fruit and vegetables, but who rely on WIC grants and food stamps that are continually on the budget chopping block from the Congress. As a mother herself, Hillary must know that one makes the best decision for the entire family. Sometimes the best decision is to buy food that is affordable and will last until the next paycheck, but that's not necessarily the healthiest. In 2010, NPR profiled a family of four who stretched their $600 a month as far as it could go, but admitted to making unhealthy decisions to get there. Too often parents have to decide between hungry and healthy, and far too often the low cost of processed foods in our grocery stores presses us to choose to end our child's hunger pangs, not provide a healthy dinner.

I am ready for Hillary to tackle food insecurity.

The last item from Hillary's knapsack that she needs to reassess is the state of birthing and breastfeeding in the U.S. According to the Institute for Women's Policy Research, 87 percent of American women don't have access to paid maternity leave, meaning that they must return to work as soon as possible after they've used whatever paid sick or vacation leave they do have. Yet the high rate of Caesarean sections is in direct conflict with quickly returning to work since that surgery requires four to six weeks of recovery time. The U.S. has the highest rate of C-sections in the industrialized world, and it cannot all be blamed on women who are "too good to push." Rather, we need to examine the medicalization of birthing in our country as being at odds with the health needs of new mothers and their children.

The lack of paid maternity leave also has a negative impact on a new mother's ability to get into a habit of breastfeeding, which has proven health benefits for infants. For me, it took a few weeks of trying before my daughter and I got the hang of things. It is far from the most natural thing that a woman can learn. Rushing back to the workplace after having a baby can impede a woman's attempt to breastfeed her baby. While "formula babies" are fine and healthy, there are still a lot of health benefits to exclusively breastfeeding children until they are six months old.

I am ready for Hillary to tackle paid maternity leave.

I am ready for Hillary to tackle the medicalization of birthing children.

Hillary Clinton is a long-time advocate for women and children, but I know I'm not the only one ready for her to really examine her positions on these policies by taking away her privilege knapsack and asking her to readjust her view.

When Hillary says that new mothers and pregnant women need additional assistance, she's absolutely right. For me, the flaw in her logic is to suggest that this struggle comes from widespread ignorance of certain classes of mothers rather than from the complex system women must operate within and that conspires to keep them from being the best mothers they want to be. If Hillary can flip her frame of reference to see low-income women in the U.S. as already empowered, but lacking in the ability to act on their knowledge, her messaging can be tweaked in a manner that will attract more low-income women and women of color to her candidacy.

Women, especially women of color, have shown themselves to be the key to Democratic victories in recent elections. Hillary can ensure a bigger commitment from this key base on her road to the White House by creating a strategy around these issues that embraces the idea of each woman's individual power— one that won't alienate the very group of women she seems so keen on "empowering." If I could tell Hillary one thing about her campaign, it is this: Reach deep inside that knapsack, toss out classist ideas about empowering women, and grab hold of that sledgehammer. If you acknowledge the power low-income women and women of color hold inside our own knapsacks, we just might bring our sledgehammers out for you too.

Can the "She" Clinton Be Commander in Chief?

Patricia DeGennaro

First there was Geena Davis in the television series *Commander in Chief*. Then there was Alfre Woodard in *State of Affairs*. Two very accomplished women, one Caucasian and the other African-American, both portraying for voters what the first female president might look like and how she might deal with the issue most commonly associated with male power—national security. Each one is a powerful woman, both in reality and on screen. They are, however, actors. So the question remains— when will the first woman inhabit the White House and become this nation's first female commander in chief and how will she deal with our nation's security? Can we imagine what a woman "C-I-C" would look like in the real world instead of just in the realm of fiction, since the U.S. presidency is still solely a masculine institution?

There have been many examples of women heads of state in real life. Through history, women have ruled Britain, Finland, Sri Lanka, Israel, India, Pakistan, and Egypt, but no American woman has reached that level of power. Hillary Rodham Clinton came exceptionally close in 2008, and the world is standing by to see if she can make it all the way to the Oval Office in 2016. Clinton, a graduate of Yale Law School, a two-term U.S. senator, and secretary of state, has been on the political stage since her undergraduate days at the renowned, all-women's Wellesley College, where, in her freshman year, she served, ironically, as president of the Wellesley Young Republicans. Her qualifications to be president rival those of many of her male predecessors. Yet, as a female, our military-centric country still questions her ability to be America's highest commander, even with over four years of experience as the country's top diplomat under her belt.

Anyone who knows Clinton, or has seen her operate, knows she is no pushover on any issue, not even national security. During the 2008 presidential campaign, she strived to ensure that voters understood this with her campaign focusing, in part, on her national security abilities developed in the U.S. Senate as a member of the powerful Armed Services Committee. Few election watchers can forget the impact that her "3 a.m. phone call" campaign ad had on the nation, which suggested that her competitors, but mainly Barack Obama, hadn't yet put in the time in understanding the international arena. It highlighted the fact that likability and charisma were less important in a presidential candidate than what she already knew from her five years on the Armed Services Committee—that there are times when a president must unwaveringly move to defend American interests, even when it's not the popular thing to do.

Clinton is a gifted politician with extensive experience, ferocious drive, and endless determination. More precisely, Clinton is one of the most uniquely qualified candidates—man or woman—who could become commander in chief; yet, in the twenty-first century, America's paternal tendencies still give the nation pause when considering whether a woman can be our military's ultimate commander. I say it's time to put those tendencies aside.

Voters rarely question whether any male candidate has the qualifications to send troops into battle or to have access to our nuclear codes, regardless of his background. President Barack Obama had virtually no foreign policy, military, or security experience when he took the oath of office. Yes, he had lived abroad as a teen (not exactly a unique experience), and as senator he had had a short stint on the Senate Foreign Relations Committee, but that entity is tasked only with overseeing foreign policy legislation and foreign aid programs, not national security or defense. Bill Clinton, as governor of Arkansas, had even less experience or exposure to national defense or military decisions. As for George W. Bush, other than a checkered, two-year stint in the Texas Air National Guard, he had even less background in defense policy when he moved into the White House. Yet, few challenged the abilities of any of those men to be in charge of our military powers.

There's no question that Hillary has far more actual qualifications to be commander in chief than the last several men to be elected president; yet, after all she's achieved, few hesitate to wonder openly about her ability to command our nation and its military. It reminds me again of the fictional President Mackenzie Allen, portrayed by Geena Davis, who quips, "There's that whole once-a-month, 'Will she or won't she push the button thing,'" though that question should really be off the table for a post-menopausal Hillary this time around! Some critics have gone so far as to suggest that shows like the now defunct *Commander in Chief*—ones that allow American TV viewers to actually see a woman in the Oval Office, making the big decisions—are a "nefarious plot to advance a Hillary Clinton presidency."

Nefarious plots aside, the question of whether a woman is tough enough to be commander in chief is one we should not even be asking. As Hillary told the 1992 graduating class of her alma mater, Wellesley College, "As women today you do face tough choices," suggesting that there will be times in their lives that they would be unfairly judged. In her speech she told them honestly that women would be judged for not being married, for not having children, and for working while leaving children at home. Unfortunately, she failed to include the fact that women also would be judged more harshly on a decision on pushing the nuclear "button" or not pushing it in favor of finding a more diplomatic or humane way out of a national security emergency.

In her memoir *Hard Choices*, which Hillary wrote after her time as secretary of state, she recounts how often she was the only woman in the room during discussions of Afghanistan, Iraq, the War on Terror, and other complex and excruciatingly difficult military issues as she worked with President Obama and others to form U.S. policy around them, further proof of the bias against women in the world of military policy and action as a man's world only. Many women know this feeling in their own jobs, but it's even more common in the areas of military intelligence and international security policy, as I've experienced more than once. As a man, no one looks at you funny when you walk into a room for a meeting or briefing on a military matter because most people there are men. No one asks why they are there regardless of their level of experience. Yet, it's not uncommon for a woman to get a response like, "What's a pretty young girl like you doing in a nasty place like this?" as I was asked once by a man when entering a Homeland Security meeting after 9/11.

Over the years, Clinton has taken the time to learn the issues and become informed and has grasped how to shape policy with political savvy. And I'll go one step further. Clinton has used her time as senator and secretary of state to learn the issues that connect the domestic with the international. She knows that because America is the most powerful nation, it can influence other nations—positively and negatively—like no other country can. As secretary of state, she guided a new agenda to look at the world globally rather than viewing the world as segregated parts, ensuring a comprehensive U.S. purview on issues like climate change, resource allocation, and women's rights—all now important international security issues affecting America every day. While many of her critics are skeptical of her making the ultimate decisions about maintaining military superiority, one thing is for sure: Hillary Rodham Clinton is a powerhouse who has expertly tamed the Congress and certainly seems to have no problem standing tall in front of the generals, some of whom are actually women, something the current administration shows us is a must for America's next president. She has a combination of knowledge and experience that few, if any, presidential candidates have ever had.

Perhaps even more importantly for our media-driven election cycles, voters have now seen images of what a woman commander in chief might look like, through the now-famous image of Hillary sitting on a military plane, Blackberry in hand, thanks to the wildly popular Tumblr site "Texts from Hillary." One of the photo mash-ups included one with President Obama texting Hillary with the message, *Hey, Hil, Whatcha doing?* Her reply? *Running the World.* Yes, the now-defunct site was parody, but it was a huge online hit, and those images of Hillary, looking very much like a woman in charge—looking like a commander in chief—are firmly implanted in our cultural political memory.

As the world continues to spiral into chaos, whoever becomes the next president will arrive at the White House with no peace dividend like the one Bill Clinton inherited in 1992. Since his White House departure in January of 2001, the U.S. went head-first into two long wars in Afghanistan and Iraq, leaving shattered families and a huge deficit to the American people. Both interventions continue to plague this country because neither has truly ended. Poorly managed by two consecutive male administrations, these invasions are pulling U.S. forces back to Iraq, keeping them in Afghanistan longer than imagined and exposing the world to a dangerous rise in extremism.

More recently, Russia has invaded two countries with no consequence. There is social and political unrest in neighboring Pakistan, India, and Kashmir and, well, if you take a good look, the unrest is pretty much across the globe. North Korea is directly challenging U.S. cyber-security. The terror threats from ISIS continue to grow in Syria, Iraq, and around the world. There is still no Israeli-Palestinian peace. In Africa, we have Boko Haram, Al Shabab, child soldiers, and Ebola. Egyptian and Syrian demonstrations spiraled North Africa, the Middle East, the Gulf, and near Asia into a region now struggling with brutal Salafist fundamentalists, Al Qaeda offshoots, and drones. Plus, the world is grappling with a migrant crisis not seen since World War II.

Yikes.

Is *anyone* really ready to manage all this?

It is hard to translate the complexity of today's world into solid policies and implement them. America needs a strong leader who is irrepressible and not afraid to wield both diplomatic and military power. Would Hillary Rodham Clinton be better suited to do that than any other candidate in 2016? Given her foreign relations experience compared to most others who have tossed their hats in the ring, the answer is a resounding, "Yes!"

Clinton knew as secretary of state she would have to align herself and her policies with other agencies in a whole-of-government approach. A keen leader knows that it takes everyone to run a country, not just a few. She understands it is important to engage others, which too many of her predecessors have failed to understand. As commander in chief she would remind us that we cannot continue to rely on our military while ignoring our diplomatic, political, and economic strength. And given her experience, she's ready to do that on day one, if elected, with no worry of the usual presidential learning curve.

Hillary put it best in her own words:

> To succeed in the twenty-first century, we need to integrate the traditional tools of foreign policy—diplomacy,

development assistance, and military force—while also tapping the energy and ideas of the private sector and empowering citizens, especially the activists, organizers, and problem solvers we call civil society, to meet their own challenges and shape their own futures. We have to use all of America's strengths to build a world with more partners and fewer adversaries, more shared responsibility and fewer conflicts, more good jobs and less poverty, more broadly based prosperity with less damage to our environment.

The United States is in a weakened position on today's international stage, not because it is inherently weak, but because it has squandered influential relationships with allies; engaged with adversaries like Iran, North Korea, and now Yemen; and forgotten about supporting a more robust diplomacy focus. Therefore, America lacks its historic weight in shaping a more prosperous, peaceful, and stable globe. Clinton knows this—in a way none of her Democratic competitors do—and as secretary of state she struggled to rekindle relationships laying the groundwork for a more engaged U.S. policy agenda in the future, for whoever becomes the next president.

In her testimony to Congress as outgoing secretary of state she repeatedly reminded us of the need for a "whole of government" solution and "friendship" diplomacy—strong relationships—ones that go beyond exclusively military to military. This means talking, engaging, putting peace before war, and, yes, making hard choices. If those valuable skills are recognized, thereby putting Clinton in the White House, she will not only make a great "first woman" president, she'll make America's most successful commander in chief. And, finally, we won't have to rely only on fictional versions for us to see what a woman commander in chief looks like.

Preaching the Social Gospel: Hillary's Mighty Fortress

Anne Born

> *A mighty fortress is our God,*
> *a bulwark never failing;*
> *our helper he amid the flood*
> *of mortal ills prevailing.*
> —Methodist hymn

What fascinates me about twenty-first century politics is the chance to examine what in the name of all that's holy would prompt a normal American adult to pursue such a career? Why do you want to be governor of this state? What makes you think you can be the voice of so many different individuals in my town? And what would make you be so desirous of the Oval Office that you would sacrifice any hope of sleeping in, toasting bagels, and working on *The New York Times* crossword puzzle on a rainy Sunday morning for the next four, or if you're lucky, eight years?

Preferring to apply what I call the Stanislavski Method of running for office, I find myself asking, "What's Hillary's motivation?" Like fledgling actors in a scene study workshop who confront the amateur director telling them arbitrarily to cross down left in the middle of their monologue, what's *her* motivation? What makes Hillary want to run? And then, do I want to give my vote to Hillary Clinton? Perhaps I do—but not without making peace with a couple of key issues, not the least of which is the separation of her church and my state.

Because once I come to grips with your motivation to take that first step into the next political arena, dear Hillary, you will have to spend the rest of your days convincing me not only that your motives are genuine and pure—well, pure enough—but that you are the one to represent me and my children—and our future—without trying to sell me on *your* future. When I vote for you, in effect, I give you my voice, and when you speak, you will speak for me, and even when I cannot verbalize exactly what it is that I need and want from you, I will put my trust in you that you will act in my best interest.

Hillary Clinton, former First Lady, former U.S. Senator from the State of New York, and former secretary of state, is also a former Methodist Sunday School teacher. While it is certainly not extraordinary that a woman who grew up to be an accomplished lawyer and public servant would have taught Sunday School at some time in her past, it is specifically in her discussion of that religious context that we learn the most about Hillary's views on family, the role of adults in the lives of children, and her vision on how best to go about raising children to become effective social actors—with a lot of prayer and the help of God, of course, using her own upbringing as a good example.

But that reference to her own childhood reminds me of *The Honeymooners, I Love Lucy,* and the "I Like Ike" buttons my grandfather wore. Can revisiting this simple 1950's rosy view of the family be what prompted her to throw her matching pillbox hat into the ring? And can she really take this glow and spread it around a twenty-first century voting public so that we all buy into her brand of social good based in devout and ever-present religious faith?

There is no way to fault her for wanting to do good in the

world, but I wonder if I can marry up my precious future with her lifelong need to act courageously and tirelessly on my behalf. After all, what does she have to offer me once I've already got lots of meaning in my life? What could she possibly restore in terms of old-fashioned American moral values when my friends, my family, and I have spent our collective lives teaching our children to be socially responsible citizens?

In 1993, then a first-term First Lady, Hillary gave a speech at the Liz Carpenter Lecture Series on Civil Society in Austin, Texas, that has come to be known as her "Politics of Meaning" speech. She described America in Rabbi Michael Lerner's terms of "alienation and despair and hopelessness," she called for a new politics of meaning defined by social responsibility, and she said more work was needed toward a "society that fills us up again and makes us feel that we are part of something bigger than ourselves."

So many political speeches are preached to the choir, written deliberately to speak to the needs and fears of the listeners in the room, so it's clear what Hillary was saying, in effect, was two-fold: the Republican Bush years left us all feeling empty, unfulfilled, and yearning for deeper meaning not only in American society but in our personal lives, and the Bill Clinton presidency was poised in that pivotal moment in the spring of 1993 to provide all kinds of meaning, with God's help, of course.

I'm not sure pursuing the "politics of meaning" will find the same welcome ears in 2016 that were found in Austin and Washington in 1993. If I were writing her speeches, I'd stop short of telling us—the 99 percent—that we live empty lives because, regardless of her years of selfless public service, Hillary Clinton is situated firmly these days in the one percent. Yet, regardless of the political cartoons, the America I see today is filled with families whose lives are both complex and meaningful. America today embraces yoga and meditation, values reducing waste, supports a variety of creative and helpful after-school programs, invents so many ways to donate clothes and food to the less fortunate among us that in the end, there are fewer less fortunate. Cancer- and AIDS-related deaths are way down, in part, because we have supported so many events that raised both awareness and funds for research. I'm just not sure how you could come off the Obama two-term Democratic presidency telling people that they need to bring themselves up now to a higher, more fulfilling social plane.

Perhaps it was something in the Clinton White House of the 1990s that provided the fertile field for the higher level of social responsibility that I see now, and perhaps God did summon Hillary to public service and ultimately to make the call "to remold society by what it means to be a human being," as she said in Austin over two decades ago. What will be interesting to see as her political future takes shape is how she will be able to compete with someone like U.S. Senator Elizabeth Warren, who has centered her brief career in public service on finance reform, or U.S. Senator Bernie Sanders, who worries that we aren't even discussing the issues that should demand our attention. If Hillary focuses on striving for the greater good, on that remolding, it could be enough to drive a successful presidential campaign, but when you scratch the surface and you find it's become a campaign based in her personal need to "lead us out of this spiritual vacuum," as she described her view of 1993 America, you might back away and say, you know, I'm good. If I really wanted the Age of Aquarius, I would still be wearing fringe and bell-bottoms.

But that was then and this is now. So is a twenty-first century Hillary any different when it comes to her take on politics and spirituality? In April 2014, Hillary spoke to the United Methodist Women Assembly about "faith in action" and the social gospel, which prompts her need to be the active and working advocate for children and families. I do not fault Hillary's big goals. Bigger is, after all, sometimes better. And I realize that she was

again preaching to the choir at this event, all the while reminiscing about her confirmation class at the church she attended as a
young girl in Illinois, remembering fondly how she would watch
her father praying at night, her mother working at the church in
various volunteer activities, and focusing on how it framed her
growing up. I just can't see this kind of organized religion-based
delivery going as far with her liberal Democrat supporters as it
has in the past. I don't think this is going to work for her. When
played out on a larger scale, when she "takes her social gospel
out into the world," I can honestly say I don't care all that much.
It starts to make me nervous, and she sounds out of touch.

I'm delighted that her Methodist faith has pushed Hillary
Clinton to work for the greater good in American society and
on the broader world stage. It's easy to see that working for her
extended congregation gives her both tremendous personal
strength as well as immense personal satisfaction. You could say
her advocacy becomes the embodiment of her "bulwark never
failing." But while this makes her strong and satisfied, I can't
say that it works for me as much as it's clearly working for her.
And if it's not working for me, how many other voters will feel
the same? I'm much happier with a public servant who keeps his
or her religious life—or even the lack of a religious life—private.
And while speaking about your life as a girl might have been a
winning strategy with political audiences in the 1990s, I'm not
willing to listen to it now. Too many twenty-first century voters
now will not be able to relate to her quaint family stories about
rising to the middle class surrounded by loved ones who had the
luxury of going to church more than once a week.

We should all want to do good because doing good is fundamental to sustaining a civil society, not because one organized
religious group ordains it. You know, dear Hillary, I've got my
own mighty fortress, and I need some critical distance from
yours.

The Responsibility of Privilege
Lisa Solod

At ten, I was the only kid in fourth grade that showed up with a "Lyndon Johnson for President" button pinned to my blouse. At twelve, I chose my college after accidentally stumbling onto a campus-wide silent vigil for the Cambodian war dead. At sixteen, a friend and I silk-screened George McGovern's photograph onto T-shirts and went to rallies for him, even though I was still two years away from voting. By that time I was also calling myself a feminist and had learned how to turn a boy down for a Saturday night date without lying that I had to wash my hair. I list those moments because I have always bought into the notion that the personal is political. My passion for politics, activism, feminism, and equal rights has not wavered in more than 40 years. But by 2008, I had also grown jaded enough to think that a man still had a better chance than a woman to be elected president, even in the twenty-first century. And, to me, Barack Obama looked like the most winning Democrat, which is why I supported him over Hillary Clinton in 2008.

Does that make sense? It does to me. The U.S. is long overdue for a woman president, just as it was long overdue for an African-American one; just as it is long overdue that race, religion, and gender shouldn't matter at all when choosing candidates. But we know today more clearly than we ever have that old, rich, white men by far outnumber candidates who are still considered outside the margin. The power broker candidates and those who fund them come from the same small group that has always run the country, no matter the party. I wasn't sure that would change with candidate Clinton two presidential election cycles ago, given that her connection to the old guard was pretty powerful, but I thought it *might* change with candidate Obama.

For me, the fact that Obama was black was a nice addition to what I considered his qualifications. I felt I could overlook the fact that he was another man because he was outside the usual privileged halls of power, even though he'd been a U.S. senator for two years when he announced his candidacy. Well, we thought he was an outsider. Either way, candidate Obama was intelligent but accessible, reasonable but passionate; he excited me. He was the first candidate to do so since Bill Clinton, and I think that much of the rest of the country felt the same way.

Is it naïve to wish to be excited by presidential candidates? Is this a leftover feeling from too long ago when John F. Kennedy's Camelot crumbled and the world took a dark turn? One that we have to give up to be more politically practical and that we might have to give up to elect our first woman president?

Hillary Clinton did better in 2008 than any woman who has ever run for president. She was the first woman to ever win a presidential primary contest, so perhaps now that enough people seem vocally tired of men in general, black or white, running the country, we may actually be ready for a gender switch, if just to see if a woman would really run our country differently. Perhaps it is time to see if a woman can screw things up less badly than a man. We started with full faith in Obama, but we let him go off script; despite the things he's gotten right, he disappointed a lot of us. But can anyone do better? Is our faith in any candidate to do what he or she promised in a campaign realistic?

And if we are to support a woman, the question remains: *Which* woman? Will any woman do? Perhaps for Republicans, who ran Sarah Palin as vice president in 2008, and who illustrated the old adage that women will have achieved success as a gender when mediocre women are as successful as mediocre men. But not for Democrats. We want someone truly qualified. So this time around, the smart money is on Hillary Clinton. But I worry that we might just be giving in. Are many of us supporting her because she has the amazing power to not give up? Because she is as tenacious as she is intelligent? Or are we giving in to the notion that Hillary's trajectory was planned long before we even knew her name: that she has been on the inside long enough to know how to play the game and win?

Democrats need a candidate who can *win*, not just one who excites our passion and our desire for a Pollyanna what-if. We saw how that turned out with George McGovern in 1972. He was the famously liberal, anti-Vietnam war candidate who sank like a stone. As a result of Democrats' ideological fervor, we ended up with Richard Nixon being reelected.

So Democrats can't run just *any* woman. But how then do we reconcile what we want with what we can *have*? Or, specifically, what we will be *allowed* to have given the current political climate? Are we willing to let go of a little excitement and accept a woman whose background of privilege is similar to those of so many men we've elected?

Former Maryland Governor Martin O'Malley, a Democrat, was quoted in a November 2014 *New Yorker* article entitled "The Inevitability Trap" as saying that his own (then not yet announced) run for the presidential nomination would be predicated on the notion that "people want to be inspired." And he's right. That is why Barack Obama took the nomination from Hillary Clinton in 2008—he inspired voters. But if some of us are disappointed in Obama's inability to put many of his inspiring words into action, do we expect that Hillary can succeed where he could not? In today's political climate, can *anyone*? Is it possible in this fractured, torn, and wounded world to be inspired by a politician anymore? Or are we too cynical, too weary; have we been let down too many times?

In a masterful and scathing 2014 *Harper's Magazine* article entitled "Stop Hillary!" journalist Doug Henwood states that the case for Hillary "boils down to this: She has experience, she is a woman, and it's her turn." For some voters, that's enough. And theoretically it should work. Hillary *does* have experience, both domestic and abroad. She is indeed a woman. And that upstart Barack Obama usurped her turn in 2008, when America decided it was more ready for a black *man* than it was for a woman of any color.

Part of me agrees that it *is* Clinton's turn. She is, after all, no worse than all the presidents we've had in the past and is a much better possible president than many of them have shown to be. While many people talk about Hillary's "inevitability," I wonder whether that is just another form of the power and privilege from whence so many prior presidential candidates have come. If it is, she needs a way to acknowledge that without alienating voters.

If we return to the idea that feminism will have reached its apotheosis when a mediocre woman rises as high as a mediocre man, then it is indeed Hillary's turn. Because, really, Hillary is far more than mediocre; she is educated, thoughtful, and intelligent in ways that too many Republican candidates and far too many members of the House and Senate (in both parties) are not. But she is also a political animal. And as Henwood points out, she has been preparing for major political office for most of her life. Are we ready to allow a woman with that kind of political ambition to be elected in the same way as men with political ambition are?

I share Hillary's fervor. I understand that she really believes she can lead us. But unlike those of us whose idealism has been tempered yet never completely disappeared, and who still hope for a candidate who can channel our idealism, Hillary is very wily: she has always been more of a pragmatist than an idealist. Her pragmatism has, in fact, made her as successful as she is. An idealist would have never accepted the position of secretary of state from the man who squelched her dreams. But Hillary saw it as a logical step toward her own ambitions and was prepared to bide her time.

* * *

When I was making calls for candidate Obama in 2008, I ran into profound ignorance and prejudice wrapped up in innocent questions, such as: "Why can't the president just get things done all by himself?" and "I think Obama is a smart man but I just can't vote for a black candidate." To the first questioner I explained the three branches of government, wondering where the woman was on the days that must have been taught in her high school civics class. To the second woman who told me, in a mellifluous Southern accent, that her upbringing and years (she was ninety-two) prevented her from voting for Obama (apparently because of his race), I merely sighed.

Despite this idiopathy, Obama won. But with his win he opened up societal rifts we all knew were there, that were just under the fabric of our "polite" American society. Some Republicans claim that his presidency brought back racism in our country, which is just plain silly to suggest. He hasn't, of course; it would be just as silly to suggest that Republicans did. Similarly, a Hillary presidency won't bring back sexism and gender issues from where they lie semi-dormant, because they are not and never have been dormant. But her candidacy is as problematic as Obama's was, for many of the same reasons. Yet none of them are reason enough *not* to vote for her. Nor, I think, is her "inevitability."

So is Hillary then the inevitable candidate? And if she is, can Democrats, both men and women, idealists and pragmatists, the world weary and the war weary, those who really yearn for Bernie Sanders or Elizabeth Warren or someone else who is more progressive or liberal than Hillary will ever be—as many

Democrats did with McGovern when his primary opponent was the more center-of-the-road Hubert Humphrey—get behind her just because she seems to have the greatest chance of winning? Yes. I think so. And that's a good thing. Ultimately, Democrats need a winner, even another flawed one. Even a privileged one.

At this juncture if Hillary Clinton and Jeb Bush (if he clears the large and unwieldy group of GOP presidential wannabes) are the two candidates who emerge from the primaries with the most power, we will once again face a choice between two American "royal" families who have dominated politics since the 1990s—two families whose privilege as political insiders cannot be denied.

The country as a whole seems to be leaning more and more to the left in terms of issues like gay marriage, universal health care, gun registration, and racial and gender equality, not to mention marijuana legalization, and an end to the so-called and completely ineffectual war on drugs. Punishing the bankers is also something most Americans seem to buy into; but will they support a truly left-wing candidate who advocates for that? Or do they prefer Hillary, Republican Lite? A candidate Elizabeth Warren could do something about that before the presidential race heats up; she could prove to be a formidable "opponent" on the issue of banking money in campaigns who can excite many progressives, even if she isn't running. And then, of course, there is Vermont Senator Bernie Sanders, the only old white man that even people who are sick of voting for old white men will happily vote for. His record as an independent progressive is impeccable, and he too wants to get money out of politics, punish bankers, and rebuild the middle class.

And yet, with all the foreign turmoil brewing daily, it seems that intelligent Americans want to elect a president who has knowledge in that arena, who knows the players, doesn't have to start from square one with understanding foreign policy or creating the delicate relationships our country has with foreign leaders, one who isn't afraid to speak his or her mind. Clinton has that covered in a way few presidents, save perhaps for George H.W. Bush, or presidential candidates before her have ever had. Even with all her qualifications, I still believe that the responsibility of privilege Hillary brings to the table is paramount. She needs to acknowledge it, own it, and embrace it as a positive. Clinton has had a very lovely life: she has dodged the scandals that plagued her husband's administration, shot down those who think her marriage is either a sham or an embarrassment, raised a smart and successful daughter who has made her a grandmother in the knick of time—just that image alone softens some of her rougher edges. She is a survivor and a thriver. But she can't be "inevitable" unless and until she acknowledges her place of privilege and owns up to that with the American public.

Yet I find something careless about her: that same carelessness that characterizes the very beautiful, the very rich, the very powerful. She shares their unwillingness to really fight hard for those who have less, have fewer chances, and have little hope. She comes from a place of power, even if it was forged by her own self, which most Americans cannot identify with. It is hard to garner much enthusiasm for a candidate who, despite her gender, seems an awful lot like everyone else who has ever run the United States. So once again, sadly, it feels like we are left to choose a candidate who doesn't quite measure up to our hopes.

Hillary's Age as Shorthand Sexism
Froma Harrop

Should Hillary Clinton become the Democrats' presidential nominee, we're going to hear a lot of talk about her age, cushioned in earnest-sounding concern and thinly-veiled sexism, just as we did in the months leading up to her official announcement of her candidacy. On November 8, 2016—our next presidential election day—Clinton will have just turned 69. That would be the age of Ronald Reagan when he entered the White House. (Actually, Reagan was only weeks away from his 70th birthday when he was sworn in as president.)

To keep this conversation honest, let's note that candidate Reagan encountered doubts about whether he was too old to be president. During a debate with Democrat Walter Mondale, a reporter asked the age question. Reagan famously responded, "I am not going to exploit for political purposes my opponent's youth and inexperience." That pretty much ended that line of discourse.

Eight years ago, when Clinton was vying with Barack Obama for the Democratic presidential nomination, the contrast between the cool youthful male senator from Illinois and the older female senator from New York could not have been made more explicit. Though not (entirely) his fault, the less-then-mature supporters in the Obama liberal camp provided some of the more outrageous remarks of the season.

Among the worst was "I'd rather vote for a black man than a post-menopausal woman." That's the level the conversation fell to—a non sequitur in addition to a slur against older women. Only marginally more sophisticated was a remark by celebrity philosopher, the late Christopher Hitchens. When he dismissed Clinton as an "aging and resentful female," the leading Republican candidate at the time was Mitt Romney, three months her senior. Hitchens said not a word about Romney's age, although he did impale the Republican's Mormonism with his trademark vitriol. And Rush Limbaugh rose, fell, or slithered sideways to the occasion with this crude remark enclosed, weasel-style, in a question: "Will Americans want to watch a woman get older before their eyes on a daily basis?"

It's now eight years later, and Hillary, like the rest of us, is eight years older. Gearing up for another presidential slugfest, Republican voices are hot on the topic of her age. For example, Mike Huckabee on Fox News said about a second Clinton run, "She's going to be at an age where it's going to be a challenge for her." At around that same time, Huckabee sponsored a great leaders tour linking Reagan with Margaret Thatcher and Pope John Paul II. "God raises extraordinary leaders for extraordinary times," Huckabee said. Did Huckabee think age was a problem for Reagan? Clearly not.

Over at *The Wall Street Journal*, political writer Gerald Seib lamented the Democrats' lack of "fresh young leaders," a jab not only at Hillary Clinton, but also at Nancy Pelosi and Harry Reid, both 74 at the time of the writing. It's a good thing for our country that Republicans weren't demanding "fresh young faces" when they made Abraham Lincoln their presidential candidate in 1860. Lincoln was 51 at a time when 51 was considered a rather advanced age. And "fresh face" was not a description easily applied to Lincoln ever.

As for Clinton, nonpartisan pundits are onto the age topic, and in some cases, tripping over a line that feels sexist to me. For example, the esteemed political analyst Charlie Cook wrote a column in 2014 titled "Is Hillary Clinton Too Old to Run?" that, frankly, set me off. Let's make something clear. The age of presidential candidates is a valid concern to the extent that age can relate to health and capacity. But Cook raised flags when he noted in his column that Clinton could be challenged for the nomination by Vice President Joe Biden—without mentioning Biden's age. Biden is five years older than Clinton. If her age were a concern, why wouldn't Biden's be even more of one? After all, age was the subject of the piece.

Furthermore, if health is the subtext here, why not look at the entire picture? If I were an insurer, I'd rather be covering a fit, 69-year-old Hillary Clinton than a seriously overweight, 54-year-old Chris Christie. (So worrisome was the New Jersey governor's heft that he reportedly had lap-band surgery in 2013 to forcibly shed pounds.)

Anyhow, I criticized Cook's gender-selective approach to a candidate's age in a column headlined "Hillary Clinton is Too Old for What?" Fox News media critic Howard Kurtz picked up on it and wrote a post in reply titled "The age of Hillary: Is it fair to question whether she's too old to run?" Kurtz didn't think Cook was being sexist, although he said I raised a valid point. Cook reportedly told him, "The vast majority of the more than 4,200 comments [in response to my column] that appeared on National.Journal.com were anti-Clinton and among the most vitriolic that I have encountered in 28 years of column writing." Hmmmm, and the subject was Hillary's age. Of course, Cooke wasn't being consciously gender biased. And he did make some amends by subsequently penning another column titled "Is Joe Biden Too Old to Run?" Cook clearly had fallen into the cultural prejudice that perceives middle-aged women as over-the-hill while their male contemporaries remain vibrant, powerful, and sexy. Hillary's enemies pound them home by using pictures of her looking tired. And countless are the illustrations and Photoshop composites portraying Clinton as a haggard witch.

Maybe we should blame some of this on Hollywood. Tinseltown has been forbidding female characters to age realistically and with dignity since forever. In the 1967 movie *The Graduate*, Anne Bancroft was only eight years older than the woman who played her daughter, Katharine Ross. Much more recently, in the 2014 movie *Tammy*, Allison Janney played the mother of actress Melissa McCarthy, who in real life was a mere eleven years her junior. Susan Sarandon portrayed McCarthy's grandmother—with only 24 years separating them. Yes, Hollywood is real rough on no-longer-young women. It's not even very respectful of young women who are rarely the main focus but rather serve as a decorative support or reward for the male stars doing heroic things. Maggie Gyllenhaal learned this the hard way when she was told that at 37 she was too old to play the love interest of a 55-year-old male lead.

But as bad as the movie business can be, the television news programs are more damaging because they purport to offer serious political reporting. Flip through most daytime cable news, and the host formula is a grizzled male journalist with a blonde half his age. The women are rarely seasoned journalists, and they often make up for their lack of depth with aggressive questioning.

The newsmen are dressed for success, wearing ties or at least jackets, all weather appropriate, with flat shoes. The women on outlets like CNN and Fox News are dressed for submission in sleeveless outfits, no matter what the wind-chill, heels they can barely walk in, and legs exposed to well above the knee. The few on-camera female survivors into middle age are not exempt from the insulting dress code. And it hurts to see all those serial face jobs and forced blonde tresses. Some have worked like the devil to maintain superb arm tone—and succeeded—but still, they should have the right to wear a tailored jacket—as should their younger sisters. Thank God for the exception, MSNBC's Rachel Maddow. And how much more modern she looks refusing to play sex kitten.

My point here is to note that this is the news/media culture into which Hillary Clinton will again be thrust. Her dress, her hair, her physique will be constantly compared and contrasted with the sad ideal of how a woman on TV or in the movies must portray herself on air, however strong and intellectually fit she may be. As for the age part, Clinton may be already taking a page from the Reagan playbook, embracing her years rather than pretending they're not there. One can see evidence of it in her posing with and tweeting about Chelsea's baby—her new granddaughter.

Setting aside the gender angle, a growing share of the electorate is becoming anxious about age discrimination as layoffs disproportionately hit older workers. That could play itself out at the polls. And women must be sensitive to this as well. When Elizabeth Warren was organizing the Consumer Financial Protection Bureau, she talked of wanting to hire "new, young staff and train them to follow the law." Three former bank examiners sued for age discrimination when they didn't get jobs. Who can blame them?

Those in the political opposition who choose to make insolent remarks about having a grandmother as president will do so at their side's own risk. On November 8, 2016, the voters will be older than four years earlier. Most will be female. And many will be both.

Won't Let Down the Team, This Time

Lisen Stromberg

It's not every day Hillary Clinton drives up to your house and asks a favor, but unexpectedly it happened to me late one Friday afternoon in the spring of 2008.

I was standing on my front lawn trying to decide where to put the large box of outgrown toys we were planning to recycle at our annual yard sale that was scheduled for the next morning. A black town car pulled along the sidewalk and out she stepped, perfectly coiffed and wearing a cerulean blue suit that matched her bright shining eyes. I'd seen her smile hundreds, if not thousands, of times in print and on television, but the media can't capture the easy, natural warmth she exudes.

"I hate to bother you," she said, almost demurely, "but would it be possible to use your bathroom?"

Someone else might not have been able to hide their shock, but I actually already knew Hillary Clinton was in town. My neighbor, a major fundraiser for Hillary's campaign and a close, personal F.O.H, was co-hosting a large "meet and greet" the next day at a local hotel. After the yard sale, I was planning on taking my twelve-year-old daughter so she could see history in the making.

Meanwhile, Hillary was going to be spending the evening at an intimate fundraising dinner in my neighbor's home. I hadn't been invited to that event (I couldn't afford the hefty price tag), but my neighbor let me know it would be happening because the Secret Service was expected to be swarming the area. Sure enough, a man in a black suit with sunglasses stood at that very moment in front of my yard watching the empty street for whatever danger he might imagine. But he was the only one. Hillary had arrived unexpectedly early, and my neighbor was not home from work yet, hence the favor asked.

"Of course," I said to the woman so many wanted to be president, and directed her inside. While Senator Clinton took care of her needs, I went back to pricing incomplete LEGO sets and puzzles with a few pieces missing; they were worth something even if they weren't in perfect order.

With her business done, Hillary took a few moments to survey my yard. A small table and chair set I had painted with cowboy hats and horses sat next to a rack of children's clothing. A bright red Mixmaster stood on a table beside a pile of old cookbooks. On the ground there was a box filled with my outdated business suits. I hadn't taken them out to price yet; they'd be the last things to go.

"It's all so charming," she said, smiling widely with a politician's enthusiasm. Her tone could be construed as gracious, but I heard something else, something that validated why, to the surprise of my family and friends, I was not one of the many feminists who rallied behind the "Hillary for President" campaign. The truth was that something about her really just pissed me off.

I've heard it said that for women, Hillary Clinton is a kind of litmus test. For some, she is a role model whose accomplishments reveal the best of what we can be. For others, she represents a repudiation of traditional choices and values. But if you believe in equality, in reproductive freedom, and in the importance of women's empowerment, Hillary Clinton should be your dream candidate. I believe in all of those things, but in 2008, she wasn't mine.

I graduated from college in 1984 when Geraldine Ferraro was making history as the first female vice presidential nominee. I was proud to call myself a feminist and had even minored in a new field: Women's Studies. My first job out of college was at the NOW Legal Defense and Education Fund working with Gloria Steinem and Betty Friedan to ensure women's rights would be fully realized.

My generation had grown up knowing we'd come a long way, baby. We wore suits with padded shoulders and pursued careers in traditionally male fields with confidence that we could, finally, have it all. I dreamed of being a lawyer and, when my mentors told me there was nothing I couldn't be, I believed them.

Fast forward to 1994. The Equal Rights Amendment is officially dead, reproductive rights are under attack, but at least Bill Clinton has been elected president. Hillary is First Lady, and I am pregnant with my first child. Rather than become a lawyer, I have an MBA and a career in business, but I certainly do not have it all. I have an hour commute, a boss who is less than supportive, and a preemie baby. And yet, like Hillary, you can be sure no one was going to catch me having teas and baking cookies.

It takes two more pregnancies, four collective months of bed rest, and one more preemie baby for me to finally wave the white flag and say, enough already. Between a hostile work environment, a salary that barely covered day care, and a media onslaught that fueled the mommy wars, it all became too much. It was clear that the career I dreamed of having wasn't possible in the face of raising three children, even with a husband who believed it was every bit as much his job as mine. So, in 1999, I quit to put my family first and, in doing so, became what I most feared: my mother.

She was pregnant with me the same year Betty Friedan gave birth to *The Feminine Mystique*. As I grew up, my mother, who did not go to college and stayed home to raise her children, complained often of the frustrations that Friedan called "the problem that has no name."

"Don't do as I did," Mother often told me. "Go to college, get a job, and never, ever, be dependent on a man," was the message she sent. She never talked about whether she liked being a mother, but to my adolescent self, it didn't seem that she did.

Here's the thing though: unlike my mother, I was happy in the role. I loved taking my children to school, volunteering in the community, and yes, even perfecting my chocolate chip cookie recipe. I worked part-time as a marketing consultant and then became a social entrepreneur by starting a non-profit working with teachers and parents to support boys in the classroom.

And yet, I felt like a failure. Instead of rising up the ladder, I was hanging with my kids on the jungle gym. All that education, all that potential, "gone to waste." My friend, Grace, who had left a successful consulting career to be with her two children summed it up best: "There is no way around it. We're letting down the team."

We weren't alone. Millions of professional women like us were also "letting down the team" by pulling back on their careers to focus on their families. Accused of "opting out," we felt the sting of our personal deficiencies. If only we had tried harder, were more ambitious, hadn't given up so easily, we'd be the leaders our society needed. Instead, we were at home, licking our wounds, and trying to make sense of the lost fight.

When Hillary stood at my doorstep that day, she symbolized all that I was not. She was a mother, a career woman, and a feminist who would never give up. And while she claimed to support all women, it was clear to me by her tone as she looked out across my cluttered yard that she didn't respect my choices or the choices of women like me. This old-school notion of feminism was one of the key reasons I believed she wasn't the best candidate in 2008. Given that she lost in the primaries, it seems I was right.

In the early 1980s, Betty Friedan published a second book that was largely ignored by the media and was resoundingly criticized amongst feminists. In *The Second Stage*, she wrote, "I believe that feminism must, in fact, confront the family.... Otherwise, it will abort or be put on history's shelf...by its denial of life's realities for too many millions of women." In the years since her first groundbreaking book, Friedan had, rightfully, been denounced for her homophobia and elitism. So her words, true as they were, never received the attention they deserved.

When I finally read *The Second Stage*, I realized there is a new problem with no name: a bias against motherhood that occurs not only in the workforce, but also across society as a whole. This new problem speaks to the underlying internal struggles women face when they are forced to deny and/or abandon their commitment to their families. Where society used to revere the woman who stayed home to care for the household, we now repudiate that role and instead glorify women's professional success. But, much like before, that success still operates under a patriarchal paradigm that does not honor the kaleidoscope of women's dreams, desires, and ambitions. Where once we rallied to break down barriers for women in the workforce, we have failed to continue to fight for the rights of families and so have left women to struggle on their own.

Put simply, we as a society don't value parenting.

We don't value it in our public policies, we don't value it in our workplaces, and we don't value it in ourselves. Those feminists who are hell bent on "empowering" women to "lean in" to the current system are, in truth, the real ones letting down the team. By focusing on "fixing" women rather than fixing the failed system, we will never truly achieve the equality for which our foremothers fought.

As I read Friedan's book, I wondered, when are we going to demand that men be as good as women when it comes to being a parent? When are we going to move beyond focusing on changing ourselves and instead on changing the social, political, and professional landscape for all women, and men? To quote Gloria Steinem, "Women are not going to be equal outside the home until men are equal in it."

Fast forward, again. It's 2015. So much has changed and yet so much hasn't. There are more women in senior management than ever before, but we continue to lack national paid sick leave, paid parental leave, and there is no national childcare system. Flexible work options are available, but not everywhere. As for pay equity, women still only make 71 percent of what men make.

Meanwhile, I went back to school and established a second career as an award-winning independent journalist and writer. I don't have a corner office, but I have control of my time and can focus on issues that are important to me. I finally came to understand you can't have it all at once, but if you are lucky, you might be able to have much of "it" over the course of a lifetime.

Hillary went on to become secretary of state, reestablishing our country's reputation around the world. In that role, she placed the plight of women and girls front and center on the global stage. She continues to fight for reproductive freedom, is working to prevent violence against women, and has proven she is a strong advocate for family-focused policies. She also became a grandmother, and now her own daughter, ironically, has decided to pull back on her career to temporarily focus on her young family.

My guess is that Hillary and I want the same things for future generations: the freedom to choose what is right for one's self and one's family, work that is meaningful and financially rewarding, and the institutional support to have both. To accomplish this, I'd like to believe she agrees with me: women *and men* need full equality at work and in the home.

In 2008, Hillary Clinton's campaign slogan was "You can be

anything you want to be." But you can't. At least not yet. To make real change for women, men, and families, I have come to realize a good man is not enough; we need a woman in power. Hillary has proven herself to be the right woman for the job. This time, I won't let her team down. This time, she has my vote.

A 12-Step Program of Her-storic Proportions

Lisa M. Maatz

H ello. My name is Lisa Maatz, and I'm *not* a Hillary Clinton addict. That doesn't mean I'm not "ready" for Hillary, or that I don't like her, or even that I wouldn't love to have a woman as president of these United States—finally! What it does mean, however, is that Hillary must win me, persuade me, *speak* to me, just like any other candidate who is looking for my vote.

I am arguably a member of Hillary Clinton's natural base: I'm a Gen X feminist and have been a progressive activist all my life. I sincerely admire her intelligence and her accomplishments; it's difficult to be the "first" of anything, and she has been the first at so many things. Hillary is the presumptive and unquestioned front-runner in the 2016 presidential sweepstakes. But I won't vote for Hillary simply because she is a woman or because she may be the only (viable) choice in the Democratic primary. She needs to earn my vote. To do that, Hillary should keep in mind this electoral twelve-step program I've created for her:

1. Suspense is overrated. We waited far too long for a definitive answer to the question that was on everyone's lips: *is* Hillary running for president? I understand wanting to be careful and deliberate. I appreciate wanting to make a thoughtful and informed decision. I did not, however, enjoy watching

Hillary playing coy in speech after speech after she left the State Department, while an entire cottage industry of commentary developed around her candidacy. Voters want decisive candidates, and the endless "will she or won't she" didn't serve Hillary well. Please don't do that again on other issues.

2. Why do you want to be president? This is the ultimate gotcha question, and Hillary must answer it, easily and from the heart, at every campaign stop. It's a question she needs to answer with clarity and more emphatically than she did in 2008. As she campaigns, she must share a well-developed and personal message about exactly why she wants to be our president. Hillary also needs to provide a clear sense of what she would do as the leader of the most powerful country in the world. The overwhelming expectation that Hillary would run cannot be seen as the reason *why* she's running.

3. This is not a coronation. Inevitability can be viewed as entitlement, and I think this is especially true for anyone named Clinton or Bush. Hillary's candidacy was "inevitable" last time, and we all know how well that worked out for her. We are not crowning a Democratic candidate or a president. It's not healthy for the candidate, the party, or public discourse as a whole if Hillary waltzes through the primary season. Democracy means choices. As one Democratic campaign veteran fretted, "We can't have a coronation when she's handing Republicans an inquisition." This leads me to my next point.

4. Head haters off at the pass. Hillary knows what kind of "swift boat" is headed her way, and she needs to face it with dignity, with integrity, and with truth. We all know that haters are gonna hate, and that some of them will play fast and loose with the facts in their zealous quest to destroy all things Hillary. She can't stop their jibber jabber, but she and her team can avoid self-inflicted wounds that create fuel for their scorched-earth politics.

5. Transparency is your friend. One of the most stubborn raps against the Clintons is that they are an especially secretive lot. The myths and realities of that reputation are for another essay, but this perception—and its impact on Hillary's candidacy—cannot be ignored. Hillary and her team need to be transparent and accountable. A prime example of her challenges came in the form of the controversy over Hillary's State Department emails and that private server. When you've got a willing cabal of haters and detractors—not to mention a 24-hour news cycle hungry for fodder—this kind of misstep just feeds the frenzy and can make Hillary look defensive regardless of whether she broke any rules or regulations. Trying to rationalize decisions by pointing fingers at others—*a la* Colin Powell who supposedly did the same thing with his State Department emails—isn't the best tactic, though I understand the temptation given the double standard by which women politicians are often judged. As a candidate, it would be very tough on her if she had another episode like that one. Voters have had enough of politicians behaving badly; we need to see Hillary rise above the fray.

6. Run toward your experience with prior administrations. Hillary is an extraordinarily well-qualified candidate. For good and for ill, she also is associated with two polarizing presidential administrations. Hillary must distinguish how "Clinton 45" will be different and better than "Clinton 42" and "Obama 44," but she can't do it by running away from Bill or Barack. She was a critical part of both administrations, and she needs to own it. Voters want to know what she would do if she were in charge, but they don't like critiques that smack of disloyalty. Hillary can be her own woman and still align herself with the best of previous administrations.

7. Be genuine and authentic. It's often said that people vote for the person they most want to have a beer with, which proved to be true with George W. Bush. This adage goes to a key point: people vote for candidates they like. Often it's just that simple. Voters not only need to hear about Hillary's policy priorities, but we also need to know why these issues matter to her. She needs to let us get to know her, not just her resume. Is there a gender stereotype at work here? You bet your ballot there is! But since we're unlikely to solve that cultural obstacle by 2016, Hillary needs to try to make it work for her. As insiders predicted, Hillary's campaign began with a short "jump start" tour to give her a chance to mingle with voters in small and more personal settings. That was one smart idea. I want to witness her delight in her newly minted grandma status *and* hear her answer questions like the seasoned secretary of state she is. The personal will ever thus be political.

8. Run as a woman. Hillary should embrace the "her"-story-making facts of her candidacy with joy and vigor, rather than trying to tone them down as she did in 2008. I want to see her revel in those eighteen million cracks in the highest glass ceiling. But even more importantly, Hillary needs to talk about her passion for addressing the critical policy issues facing women and families, issues she understands so well. Polls have shown, over and over again, that voters want to hear candidates talk about these "kitchen table" economic issues. She can be an excellent messenger for the fact that women's issues are everyone's issues; that addressing them is not only the right thing to do, but also the smart thing to do to grow the nation's economy. As secretary of state, Hillary made women's issues a serious priority, and her popularity soared. Her last presidential campaign tried to whitewash her feminism, and it was a mistake.

9. Work for every vote, and . . . Hillary needs to be in it to win it. Her energy, her message, it all needs to underscore that she is working for every vote and that every voter matters. The perceived lack of viable competition cannot be allowed to water down her primary effort. It won't serve our nation well if Democrats give the impression that Hillary is skating to the nomination. She needs to run an accessible, retail campaign not just in Iowa and New Hampshire but nationwide. Hillary should do meet-and-greets, round tables, and relaxed town halls that will allow her to talk directly to voters. She needs to recapture that down-to-earth manner that emerged toward the end of her last campaign. And if her Democratic competition remains relatively low-key, she needs to run a primary that rallies her base with an eye toward the general election.

10. Don't take women voters for granted. Most women want to see a woman president in their lifetimes. But I don't think that most women want a woman president simply so we can check off that historical box. It's critical that Hillary illustrate to women voters of all ages, parties, and persuasions how her forward-thinking plans and steady leadership will improve the everyday lives of our families—and she needs to repeat it over and over and over again.

11. Have a multi-generational and multi-cultural approach. Women age 50 and over are strongly inclined to support Hillary because she's well qualified *and* a woman. While Millennials were less enthusiastic about her candidacy last time around, those same Millennials are now eight years older, many with families of their own. Hillary's successful tenure as secretary of state, as well as her social media presence, has helped her begin to bridge that generation gap. The growing strength of the demographic called the "Rising American Electorate"—unmarried women, people of color, and voters under 30—is Hillary's ticket to 1600 Pennsylvania Avenue. Her campaign staff, her surrogates, and her message must all reflect and continue that progress. Hillary's 2016 run for the White House must be a campaign of the new millennium: inspirational, inclusive, and innovative.

12. Last but not least: Remember that "liberal" is not a dirty word. Here are just a few of the definitions of the word liberal at Dictionary.com:

> *Liberal:* adj. *1. favorable to progress or reform, as in political or religious affairs. 2. noting or pertaining to a political party advocating measures of progressive political reform... 7. free from prejudice or bigotry; tolerant.*

As Hillary well knows from her 2008 campaign, labels can be used as weapons to hurt or discredit, but they can also be used to rally the troops. Being a "liberal" is one label Hillary should embrace. There's a reason why there continued to be a concerted effort for a "Draft Elizabeth Warren for President" campaign for so long, and it's all about voter uncertainty on Hillary's left flank. Voters need reassurance that her New Democrat ways have been tempered by the Wall Street collapse, spiraling student loan debt, the foreclosure crisis, and the outsourcing of American jobs—not to mention mounting income inequality. The Democratic wing of the Democratic Party is looking to Warren as its leader, but Hillary needs their energy, their allegiance, and their money to win in 2016.

Hillary Clinton knows she's in for a grueling campaign. Her challenge will be to stay focused on her message rather than getting caught in the rhetorical traps of the opposition. In doing so, Hillary will be able to demonstrate that she not only wants to be our president, but that she is the best candidate for the job.

FLOTUS, SCOTUS, POTUS, SCHMOTUS

Nancy Giles

Here's the thing about Hillary Clinton. She rarely says "uh," "you know," or "like." Which I find a little unnerving. She went through a lot of hairstyles as First Lady, which I can relate to (not the being First Lady part, but the going-through-a-lot-of-hairstyles part). And she's probably the smartest person in any given room. Which I can't really relate to, and I also find a little unnerving, and I'm sure is a burr in most folks' butts.

And now Hillary is considered the inevitable Democratic nominee for president in 2016. And okay, I admire her I guess, and she's definitely qualified for the job, but when I think about a woman running for the White House, the person I immediately think of is Shirley Chisholm: her guts, her smarts, her overbite that gave her that distinctive lisp from the back of her mouth. I was too young to appreciate all of that back in 1968, when Shirley was the barrier-breaking first black congresswoman in the United States, and then four years later when she had the audacity to run for president of the United States. And she was from Brooklyn, and okay, I was from Queens, but I had cousins in Brooklyn! And Shirley didn't just happen to have a husband who had already been president of the United States!

The thing is, I wasn't paying attention to politics in the '90s because living in Los Angeles and acting on a TV series had me pretty distracted. I was more concerned with getting a parking spot with my name on the curb somewhere near our soundstage. (Parking proximity at Warner Brothers was hugely political.) So other than the fact that I was a Democrat and Bill Clinton was a Democrat, and Clinton/Gore won the election, what did I know? I knew I didn't like Hillary's outfit during the inauguration ceremony. I watched her, Bible in hand, Bill repeating the oath of office, and I thought, *What is with that hat?* Even her scarf looked dowdy. "She looks like his mother," my mom said long-distance while we watched the ceremony on different coasts. And she did, except why were we stuck on what Hillary was wearing? Because that's what we do. Women look and comment about how other women look, from women they pass on the streets to celebrities, politicians, and of course our First Ladies. We check each other out from hair weave to high heels. We just do.

My disdain for her '90's-era dowdiness aside, I voted for Hillary Clinton in 2000 when she ran for a Senate seat in New York. She was the first First Lady to run for public office, she was hands down the smarter, more experienced candidate, and, if elected, she'd be the first woman senator from New York. It was a no-brainer. So I was stunned that some New York women, women I respected, said there was no way they'd vote for Hillary because *"she should have left him,"* or *"when she stayed I lost all respect for her,"* or *"I don't trust her judgment since she didn't leave him."*

Huh?

What about her accomplishments? Her incredible resume? None of that mattered. These women were angrier at Hillary for staying with Bill than they were at Bill for being a liar and cheater and a cheater and liar again, this time with a college intern. What did Hillary do? Were these women projecting their own unhappy experiences onto her? How was she the bad guy, and not Bill? I mean, if we're going full-tilt soap opera, can't we keep our villains straight?

Is that what women do?

But wait. It gets better. Eight years later some of these same women friends did a complete 180 and were rabid in their support of Senator Hillary Clinton's run for president. Like, if you were a woman, you had to support Hillary. You just had to— no ifs, ands, or buts. In fact, how could you not? She had the pedigree, as a combo feminist icon/First Lady/first "wronged woman." Her struggles were our struggles. It was her turn. That first black president thing might be cool, but gender trumps race, don't you understand? And Hillary represented all of us. Wait. Who's "us"?

So even though I supported Hillary in her senate campaigns, I had a problem with that "all of us" thing, just like I always had a problem with the phrase "women and blacks," because what people really meant when they talked about "women and blacks" was white women and black men, and where exactly did I fit into that equation? Yes, Hillary was smart and all, and by now those First Lady hats were off and she finally had a great haircut, but I was all in for Barack Obama. And I kept thinking that while Hillary had a lot to offer, Bill Clinton had already been president. Twice. So another Clinton in the White House? It seemed ... icky.

That's not meant as a dig at Hillary; I know she's very much her own woman with honors and accolades from her time as a student at Wellesley through her many years of public service, First Lady duties, advocacy for women and children and more, and as a two-term United States senator. And after a fierce presidential primary campaign (including a little crying, some *"He's not a Muslim ... as far as I know"* insinuating, and some Bill dispatching to rally the white Southern vote), when she lost the nomination to Barack Obama, she had the smarts to join his cabinet as secretary of state. (That's the CliffsNotes version.) I mean, come on. Hillary Clinton has a political resume that could choke a horse. And in my humble opinion, she was always the better politician, not Bill. Unfortunately, I can't get past the fact that Bill—her husband—has already been president. Twice. So why does Hillary need the same job he had? Is this her big, bad, public smackdown of Bill, kind of like the song from *Annie Get Your Gun*:

> *Anything you can do, I can do better*
> *I can do anything better than you*
> *(No you can't)*
> *Yes I can*
> *(No you can't)*
> *Yes I can*
> *(No you can't)*
> *Yes I can, yes I can!*

Are the Clintons' dinner conversations lacking? Or somewhere deep in her psyche, does Hillary feel like Bill "owes" her this? He does owe her—he owes her many apologies, yes. Or maybe she deserves a few affairs of her own. But this feels like an "even the score" presidency, with a dash of Veruca Salt in *Willy Wonka and the Chocolate Factory*:

Hillary: "**Bill** was President of the Oompa-Loompas. Why can't **I** be President of the Oompa-Loompas?"

Isn't there something weird about this? And can you really see Bill getting out of Hillary's way, even though he says he would? I can't. And hasn't our very recent history with presidential relatives taught us anything? The country is still suffering the disastrous effects of George W., the number two Bush and his "*I'll get Saddam for ya', Daddy*" presidency. Enough already with the family dynamics, codependent relationships, and boundary issues being played out on the political stage, and on the taxpayers' dime. You can watch those train wrecks on any of the *Real Housewives* shows. What we need is a Constitutional amendment with a one-president-per-family limit. First cousins could run for office, maybe. But no immediate family members, and only one half of one couple, be they straight or gay. You're a uniquely qualified woman, Hillary Clinton. And I wish you'd stayed on as secretary of state. You were a fearless team player. Even with all of your credentials, experience, and natural political ability, I have to walk away from you. If it's more politics you want, there are other offices you could run for—maybe Senate again? Or a governorship? Mayor of Chappaqua? But not president. I wish you'd have run for president first, and persuaded Bill to cool his heels and have your back, but it didn't happen that way. There are other worthy women with new perspectives, women without relatives who've already been president of the United States who deserve a shot.

My picks? How about Indra Nooyi, the CEO of PepsiCo, called one of "America's Best Leaders" by *USA Today*? Or Kirsten Gillibrand, the feisty junior senator from New York? Or Ursula Burns, the CEO of XEROX and one of *Fortune Magazine*'s "Most Powerful Women"? Or Samantha Power, the U.S. ambassador to the United Nations? Or voting rights advocate and former state senator from Ohio Nina Turner? Or U.S. Senator Elizabeth Warren, consumer advocate and ass-kicker of big banks?

You've served your country well, Madam Secretary. Time to let go of that bat and give someone else a chance to swing. Time to move on. I so want to see a woman elected president in my lifetime, but we need a different candidate with a fresh new perspective, with a fresh set of eyes, and without political baggage. Well, maybe a carry-on.

Hillary the Hawk?

Jaime Franchi

Hillary. Like a renowned celebrity of stage and screen, she is known simply by her first name, though it's her last that catapulted her to international recognition. But no one on any side of the political spectrum could accuse Hillary Clinton of resting on the laurels provided to a First Lady. In fact, she reshaped the role of First Lady by taking an active role in her husband's administration by digging into policy and transcending advocacy. She overcame carpetbagger status to become a U.S. senator in New York and became secretary of state in her adversary's administration after losing in a presidential primary. In short, she's earned that recognition.

Only a week after President Barack Obama's second inauguration, with immigration reform and the debt ceiling pressing, the gun control debate spiraling into ever more shrill pitches, and pointed looks into his use of drone strikes, an impatient nation decided that it was of course the time to project into an uncertain future and remark on who might be the next guy to take his seat.

"Guy," of course, is a euphemism to mean either "man" or Hillary Clinton. Beginning with the lovefest that was the January 28, 2013, *60 Minutes* co-interview with President Obama and the outgoing secretary of state, it looked to me to be the groundwork of the 2016 election season. In the way that Bill Clinton almost single-handedly ignited Obama's reelection campaign,

Obama publicly repaid that favor, recycling the loving stare that Mitt Romney employed during each of their presidential debates, implicitly raising Hillary's White House recognition level.

There is no doubt that Hillary Clinton is a force. As a woman and as a political writer, but mostly as a voter, I've kept my eye on her for years, as a cheerleader with a modicum of caution. Because what's exciting about elevating a woman as tremendously capable as Hillary to the highest office in the land is the barrier-breaking that it represents. Yet I'm not at all convinced that this particular broken barrier would extend beyond the pronouns with which we speak about our chief executive.

And that is the conundrum here. What makes Hillary precisely electable is the strength she exudes in the face of misogynists, the brilliance she possesses as a political candidate that almost casts her gender into irrelevance. Hillary has been reluctant to play the woman card. She does not tout designers. She does not pose.

She works.

As a woman candidate, Hillary will need to demonstrate the strength normally associated with candidates of the male persuasion. Therefore, her preference for military might in Syria, Libya, and Afghanistan will be played as a marked strength if she gets to the general election. Yet before that, she has to get through what many call the campaign "silly season." In the primaries, Hillary will need to appeal to progressives who are still reeling from the ugly, drawn-out ending of the longest war in U.S. history. With pressure from such progressive darlings as a vocal Senator Bernie Sanders and the brilliant Senator Elizabeth Warren, the heat will be on Hillary and will stay for a very long campaign season.

This is precisely where my Hillary support begins to break down. The most polarizing aspect of Hillary's reputation is that she is seen as hawkish. The fundamental question that needs to be asked is if the perception of Hillary as a war hawk, as one who leans heavily on military might to solve and enforce the United States' authority in the world, is exaggerated because she is female. If a man had taken many of the same positions she did as secretary of state or U.S. senator, would he be painted as a hawk or as a steel-toed man of strength?

The answer is complicated.

In a 2007 interview with *Marie Claire* Editor in Chief Joanna Coles, Hillary responded to the question of whether, as a woman candidate, she would need to be "doubly tough on the issue of war" this way:

> *No, I don't. I feel like I have to do what I believe is right. I don't think we need to have an either/or debate about the use of military force—I think you can be both tough and smart. And we haven't had that for the last six-and-a-half years. We are desperately in need of the kind of smart diplomacy that has worked for America in the past. If you use force, it should be a last resort. And it needs to be used with full understanding of the consequences. I bring the experience that I had in eight years in the White House where Bill did intervene in places like Bosnia and Kosovo but did it in a smart, effective way. George Bush—the first George Bush—also [was effective] in putting together a real coalition, not a pretend coalition.*

But does her record bear that out?

Just as it did in the run-up to the 2008 election, Hillary's position of supporting the disastrous war in Iraq continues to be an issue. Of course, hindsight being what it is, it's easy for political pundits to point to this decision, knowing unequivocally that no weapons of mass destruction would be found, that Iraqis would welcome Americans with less than open arms, and that the fall of Baghdad would take a profound and devastating toll, both in the loss of life on both sides and in the morale of the country.

Yet this decision sets a precedent for further study into the mind of a potential commander in chief. Hillary did more than raise her hand and vote "Aye" for an Iraqi invasion. She insisted that Saddam Hussein had "also given aid, comfort, and sanctuary to terrorists, including al-Qaeda members." This attempt to link Iraq with the attacks on the World Trade Center on 9/11 as a justification for war is a pock on United States military history.

In her book *Hard Choices*, Hillary addresses her Iraq War decision as one that she would do her best to learn from:

> *As much as I might have wanted to, I could never change my vote on Iraq. But I could try to help us learn the right lessons from that war and apply them to Afghanistan and other challenges where we had fundamental security interests. I was determined to do exactly that when facing future hard choices, with more experience, wisdom, skepticism, and humility.*

And yet.

Hillary, along with then Secretary of Defense Robert Gates, was also a strong supporter of the troop surge in Afghanistan led by the now-ousted General Stanley McChrystal, over the reported resistance of President Obama and Vice President Joe Biden.

And then came the conflict in Libya. Hillary promoted the airpower strike that toppled the regime, resulting in anarchy and sectarian conflict, and helped to create a breeding ground for Islamist extremists that have destabilized the region. And then she promoted the same strategy for Syria, with similar results.

So for me, the issue of Hillary's level of hawkishness is so much more complex and close to my heart, not just as a fellow woman, one who would love to support another to the highest office.

I need to consider whether I am willing to settle (again) for a candidate who has much-too-cozy connections with Wall Street, has a reputation as a war hawk, and who came late to the causes closest to our collective hearts, such as gay rights.

Yet, she is someone who just might have the experience, qualifications, and chutzpah to win this damn thing, if redistricting hasn't made it impossible for any Democrat to win for the next ten years.

This decision—a decision on whether or not to vote for Hillary Clinton—like so many before it, will be one of many "hard choices."

Is "Too Small To Fail" Hillary's Failsafe Way to the White House?

Estelle Erasmus

For the majority of her professional and political career, Hillary Rodham Clinton has rejected the purely feminine role, and she's paid a steep political price for it. When asked during Bill Clinton's 1992 presidential campaign about her life, she famously replied, to much derision, "I suppose I could have stayed home and baked cookies and had teas, but what I decided to do was fulfill my profession which I entered before my husband was in public life." Women, particularly women who had never worked outside the home, were appalled at what they felt was her dismissive insult, and it hurt her on a grand scale, even though she later won a *Family Circle* magazine bake-off against Barbara Bush, her Oatmeal Chocolate Chip recipe defeating the traditional Chocolate Chip cookie version Barbara produced. Hillary's 1996 bestselling book *It Takes a Village: And Other Lessons Children Teach Us* seemed to many to be a response to the world's judgment about how she wasn't motherly, as well as to her health care reform debacle.

That double-edged criticism continued on her book tour. She was frequently bombarded with questions about her involvement in the Whitewater and "Travelgate" controversies. And Bob Dole, the 1996 Republican presidential nominee and her husband's opponent, suggested to the country that she didn't know what she was talking about when it came to parenting, saying "…with all due respect, I am here to tell you, it does not take a village to raise a child. It takes a family to raise a child." In her 2003 book *Living History*, Hillary tried to reclaim her policy and parenting *bona fides*, contending that, "Dole missed the point of the book, which is that families are the first line of responsibility for children, but that the village—a metaphor for society as a whole—shares responsibility for the culture, economy and environment in which our children grow up."

Amidst the detritus of Hillary's spectacular failure to win the Democratic nomination for president in 2008 was her absolute resolve to not use her gender as a political scythe and her desire not to be viewed through any sort of gender lens at all. Hillary famously told audiences that she wasn't running as a woman candidate, but as the best candidate.

But Hillary's gender, pundits say, is exactly what must be used as a key element of her strategy for a 2016 White House run. It would also be her best avenue by which to extricate herself from her biggest known political liability—a connection to the Obama administration as secretary of state. In a 2014 *New York Times* article, Chris Lehane, a Democratic strategist, told the group Ready for Hillary that "being a woman translates into great politics." If that's true, what can Hillary do to capitalize on that perceived "woman" advantage in 2016 that wasn't there in 2008? The answer is this: her dedication to advocating for women and children at home and abroad, a topic that has yet to be as boldly embraced by any prior presidential candidate, male or female, in quite the same way, but that could resonate with women voters of all political stripes—women voters who, after all, decided the outcome of the 2012 presidential race, and have voted in larger numbers than men since 1980. The good news for Hillary is that she has always had an interest in early education, so focusing on these issues as a candidate will be natural for her, and voters will likely understand and respond to that.

While Hillary was First Lady, she led a bipartisan effort to establish Early Head Start and oversaw educational reforms when her husband was governor in Arkansas. Early education is certainly a hot-button issue, because even though we all want the positive results—a better future for America's children which equals a better future for America—there is a spectrum of ideas on how that should be accomplished.

In 2013, Hillary started "Too Small to Fail," a privately funded venture that is a joint initiative of Next Generation and The Bill, Hillary & Chelsea Clinton Foundation (a nonprofit which was formerly the Clinton Foundation). The Bill, Hillary & Chelsea Clinton Foundation focuses on three areas that Hillary should highlight in a campaign: early childhood development, expanding opportunities for women and girls, and improving economic development around the world. The mission of Too Small to Fail falls into her early childhood development wheelhouse with its mission to improve the health and well-being of America's children, ages zero to five, by promoting scientific research about early childhood development with the goal of reaching as many parents and business leaders as possible and motivating them to act. "It's economically irresponsible to think we can continue to thrive as a nation with a generation of kids who aren't prepared to enter an increasingly competitive global economy," said Jim Steyer, co-founder of Next Generation.

If, as most political pundits believe, Hillary is making her early education initiative a pinnacle part of her plan to win the Democratic nomination, then it's a brilliant strategy to deal with both the people who love her, as well as her haters. Whether a person is for or against Hillary on this issue, she has her finger on the collective zeitgeist which is focused on using all the tools at our disposal (positive psychology, neuroscience, and peer-reviewed studies) to build resourceful children who will move this country forward, and hopefully provide the United States with an eventual edge on the world stage. Whether or not you are a parent, and whether or not your children are preschool age, we can't ignore the fact that today's kids will be our future doctors, emergency personnel, customer service workers, computer technicians, and caretakers, so it only will benefit us to set them up to succeed. So, in essence, education has become the new economic issue, and the economy has long been the number one issue among women voters.

In a 2013 op-ed on the Clinton Foundation's website, based on a report generated by the Clinton Foundation arguing for the importance of getting parents to spend more time talking to their kids, Hillary wrote, "Studies have found that by age four, children in middle- and upper-class families hear 15 million more words than children in working-class families, and 30 million more words than children in families on welfare. This disparity in *hearing* words from parents and caregivers translates directly into a disparity in *learning* words. And that puts our children born with the fewest advantages even further behind."

Hillary's initiative is supported by a new study by the National Bureau of Economic Research that found that preschoolers whose parents received text messages with brief tips on reading to their children or helping them sound out letters and words performed better on literacy tests than children whose parents did not receive those messages.

A platform of education appeals to many women, who made up 53 percent of the vote in the last presidential election, and who feel in a time where there are laws being passed on a statewide level to reduce the rights to their bodies that their voices need to be heard on both women's and mother's rights.

As past president of the board of directors for Mothers & More, a national nonprofit founded to support the work of mothers both in and out of the home, and as the mother of a five-year-old who has attended preschool since she was two and a half years old, and who benefitted greatly on a cognitive and social level from her early education, I feel strongly that the time is now for the work of motherhood to be taken seriously, especially in a presidential campaign. With Hillary's help from Too Small to Fail, so many more women can be supported in being mothers and working outside the home for pay, without suffering economically because they have no other safe option than to stay home to take care of their kids. If she can successfully combine her education messaging with increasing how we as a society should value motherhood, she could win an impressive percentage of the women's vote and start thinking about the title "Madam President."

But early childhood education and support of mothers isn't just on Hillary's agenda. She has her party's support for her interest in early education, as well. In December 2014, President Barack Obama announced over $750 million in federal funding for early learning programs through the Preschool Development Grants and Early Head Start-Child Care Partnerships, as well as calling for the expansion of early childhood opportunities for children across the country through public and private commitments to investment in early childhood programs and research.

Although it's hard to argue with the idea of education as a pinnacle issue, Hillary has her detractors when it comes to making early education a focus for children. Claire McCarthy, M.D., a pediatrician at Boston Children's Hospital and a spokesperson for the American Academy of Pediatrics, has wondered if government is just too big to make a difference and has said, "...there's so much [that] a book and a pep talk from me can't do. They can't teach a parent to read. They can't make it so that a parent is home at bedtime, instead of working the evening cleaning shift while an older sibling or neighbor watches the child. They can't get rid of the toxic stress that pervades every family interaction."

And the criticism doesn't stop there. In the *Baffler*, a publication dedicated to cultural criticism, a skewering article by

Emmett Rensin and David Shor contends that Too Small to Fail *will* fail "...because reading to children, even young children will not necessarily make them smarter." While the authors admit there is a "wealth of data" showing a connection between reading to young children and increases in their test scores and intelligence, they claim the studies themselves are inconclusive.

Critics are missing the point that Hillary understands—there are so many communities and constituencies invested in a better education for their children that a presidential candidate with an education-meets-economy agenda will be very appealing. And that's something that has been shown to be very important to Hispanic voters—and if you win women voters and Latino voters, you win the election. Barack Obama won 70 percent of the Hispanic vote in 2012, and Hillary appears poised, with Too Small to Fail's latest partnership with Univision, the highest rated Spanish network, to get that vote, as well. For Hillary Clinton, the partnership with Univision provides not only a valuable platform with what one commentator calls "the country's fastest-growing and politically influential Hispanic community," but the owner of Univision, Haim Saban, a billionaire Democrat, has recently said that he personally supports Hillary for President. That's a powerful "in" with that voting bloc.

Hillary also has Sandra Gutierrez, the National Director of Abriendo Puertas/Opening Doors as a member of Too Small To Fail's advisory council. Abriendo Puertas/Opening Doors has created a model for honoring and supporting Latino parents and partnering with them to help their children enter school ready to learn and able to succeed in life. Gutierrez has said, "The families we work with are Spanish-speaking and 100 percent low income within federal guidelines. They're the working poor and have a great work ethic. They want their kids to have a better future and more opportunity for education than they had. We demonstrate how a household can promote early literacy practices, and it's great to work with parents when the children are so young, because that prepares them for just one step in a much larger process of family engagement."

If Hillary is elected president in 2016, becoming a "first" in the way that Barack Obama was a "first" for African Americans, she will have historic claims for her gender, so she should embrace that in a run for the White House. Not only will she be the first female president, but she will also be the first president who is also a loving mother and a doting grandmother.

Given her long-time interest in women and girls, and early childhood education, Hillary appears ready, willing, and able to finally accept both sides of her, the nurturing female and the consummate policy professional, in a way she (and the rest of the country) never did before. This acknowledgement just may be the ticket she needs to come full circle again—baking cookies and having tea—and of course nurturing our country's children—in the celebrated citadel of power itself—the White House.

What I've Learned from Hillary the Wellesley Girl

Katherine Reynolds Lewis

One of the facts in Hillary Rodham Clinton's biography that has always loomed large in my mind is her Wellesley College degree. When I was an undergraduate at Harvard in the 1990s, buses spewed Wellesley students into Harvard Square each weekend, all made up and dressed for romantic battle. They were our competition for men, and they tilted the male-female balance at the parties and clubs to put us all at a disadvantage. My female friends and I considered the Wellesley girls our sworn enemies.

At the time, I couldn't understand why any straight girl would choose to attend a women's college. I was 18, full of hormones, and eager to be in as close proximity to as many boys as possible. Plus, the young feminist in me considered it a cop-out to retreat to female-only classes and lecture halls. At the time I thought, how could you prove you were as good as—or better than—the men if you weren't going toe-to-toe with them academically?

I chose physics as my major, or my concentration, as Harvard calls it, after the boys in my freshman entryway scoffed at my decision to sign up for Physics 5. "You'll never last," they predicted. I was determined to prove them wrong and myself worthy of what I considered the finest college in the world. I assumed that anyone at Wellesley would have enrolled at Harvard if she had a strong enough academic record to win acceptance. (Can we blame my educational snobbery on youth?)

Of course, when Hillary Rodham arrived at Wellesley in the fall of 1965, a women's college education meant something entirely different than when I went off to Harvard three decades later. She was in the vanguard of young women seeking an education for an actual profession at college, not just their "M.R.S." degree. The Ivy League hadn't yet begun to admit women, so she didn't have the choice between Harvard or Wellesley, as I later did. When I talk to my mother, who is of that same generation as Hillary, she speaks of the women who attended Wellesley and other Seven Sisters' colleges as strong and independent, career-minded, and determined to change society—certainly not the idea of Wellesley girls I had in my head. Hillary's class of '69 consisted of a wave of newly-hatched Betty Friedan-era feminists being unleashed upon the world.

In the years since I graduated from Harvard with that hard-won physics degree, I've come to appreciate the nuance in these choices. My own career and life path has been far from the straight line that I envisioned when I entered Harvard. I now truly believe in the concept of "fit" over "rank" when it comes to schooling, having seen my brilliant stepdaughter blossom after she moved from a higher-ranked college with a distinctive identity to a lower-ranked one with a more accepting culture. And, as the mother of daughters, I now see the merit in carving out all-female spaces for education, debate, and building relationships—something that Hillary and her classmates apparently realized decades ago. That separation can be made on a large scale—your choice of college—or a much smaller one, such as networking groups or associations for women's advancement. I belong to several such groups now and understand their unique value, even though as a young co-ed I didn't yet appreciate them.

Today, now that I'm a little older, a little wiser, and a little more battle-tested professionally, I wonder whether there was something in the isolation of those Wellesley girls from the Harvards of the world that set them on a path of sisterly solidarity forged in a woman-only environment that creates women leaders like Hillary Clinton. Did they, as well as all the other young women who attended single-sex colleges, discover something about a potential lifelong sisterhood network that could benefit them in ways beyond reminiscing at class reunions?

While women have drawn closer to men in access to education and jobs, we still face a stubborn gap in pay and advancement. We may graduate high school and college in larger numbers than men, but from the moment we receive our diplomas, the gap begins. We receive lower starting salaries, are promoted at slower rates, and drop behind—or out—of the workforce as we reach the age of family formation and childrearing.

Much of this is due to outright or implicit bias against women and misperceptions of our suitability for the highest ranks of business and professional life, as documented by scholars such as Joan Williams, the founding director at the Center for WorkLife Law at UC Hastings College of Law, and organizations including Catalyst and McKinsey. And I would argue that even the gap that is due to women choosing to take a less-ambitious work track—"leaning out," so to speak—stems from the reality we confront of building our careers in work cultures that reward always-on employees and penalize workers of any gender who prioritize family and personal needs. Those who take the "mommy track" might make far different choices living somewhere with policies and a business culture supportive of working parents, such as Sweden or Canada.

I have seen male classmates leverage their college friendships and college-era networks into career success, forming companies together and steering business opportunities to each other over the years. I'm not sure if that happens with their female counterparts, but such back-scratching certainly hasn't been the case for me. Perhaps if I had been more open to seeing other women as allies, instead of romantic competition, I would've built stronger relationships that would serve me in my career now. Is that something those Wellesley girls intuitively knew? Or maybe I should blame my post-graduation decision to switch my focus from physics to journalism, after the opportunity had flown to join the *Harvard Crimson* or *Independent*, where I likely could have forged the kind of personal connections for later professional networking. Most likely, I was just focused on friendship for its own sake, something true to this day, and those in my closest circle have gravitated to other fields.

But the question still remains in my mind: what if the significant difference between the Wellesley girls and Harvard girls of my day wasn't in our SAT scores or GPAs? Could it have been this philosophical choice between trying to best the men at their own game, or building our own game board and writing our own rules? And did Hillary and her classmates know or somehow sense that their own paths to success or power would be better paved by immersing themselves in a community of and dedicated to women and their education?

Certainly, Hillary Clinton's career path included Wellesley ties. Wellesley friend Nancy Pietrafesa worked for Bill Clinton when he was governor of Arkansas. Hillary classmate Eleanor Dean Acheson, granddaughter of renowned Secretary of State Dean Acheson, became assistant attorney general in the Clinton administration's Justice Department. And Jan Piercy, who led the charge for a student speaker at Wellesley's 1969 commencement, was appointed to the World Bank by President Clinton and served seven years as U.S. executive director during his administration. Hillary's fiery commencement speech, the first ever by a Wellesley student, won her national attention—a spot in *Life Magazine*'s feature on the class of 1969 and a speaking invitation to the League of Women Voters—and, in a sense, launched her political career.

Looking at my contemporaries who went to Wellesley—high

school classmates, a foreign exchange program buddy, and friends I've met since then—it's obvious that they're universally well-educated, intelligent, and contributing human beings, not at all deserving of the sneers my posse and I delivered when we bumped into a gaggle of Wellesley girls at final club parties. And I sense they don't have the same questions today that I have about whether I have a harder time accessing certain college connections and networks because I am a woman who had a co-ed college experience. They know their Wellesley experience—as undergrads and beyond—was entirely devoted to their gender. While that's not enough to make me regret attending Harvard instead of Wellesley, it certainly puts one solid mark in the "pro" column for any high school senior debating her college decision.

At some point, we each must prove our worth—to ourselves, our contemporaries, and the world. Indeed, these tests are rarely final and often nerve-wracking. There's something to be said for entering into such moments with the solid support of a true sisterhood. As Hillary Rodham Clinton embarks upon another presidential run, those Seven Sisters college ties may well come in handy. And who knows. Maybe that's exactly what's needed for America to finally elect its first woman president.

The Long Road to Yes
Lezlie Bishop

In 1966, if someone had discussed the possibility of electing a woman to the White House, I probably would have assumed it would be me. I was consumed by ambition on that hot June day in Wisconsin on the Ripon College library lawn when my B.A. in Psychology was conferred. I believed then that I would accomplish *any* goal I set for myself, including becoming president.

The truth was, there would have been no one in the vicinity who would have done much more than snort and sneak an incredulous look my way if I had expressed those thoughts out loud. That particular benchmark was not expected to happen in our lifetimes.

When 2008 rolled around and Hillary Rodham Clinton, a woman of my own generation, was the presumptive nominee for president of the United States, I was squarely in her corner. Not because she is a woman. I didn't think that way. No, it was because I have admired her from afar ever since her husband campaigned for *his* presidency in San Francisco in 1992 and my co-worker/best friend dragged me to an outdoor rally where he was speaking.

Three decades ago, my friend and I knew little about either Clinton, but my friend pointed out how much she loved Hillary's headband and blonde flip. I knew the nominee's wife was very smart and had graduated from Yale Law, which appealed to me far more than her hairstyle. Even with her educational pedigree, we both liked the way HRC played the doting and approving "wifey" as she sat behind him on the platform, nodding her head where appropriate and smiling that smile of hers. That might sound odd today, but remember, it was 1992. Both my friend and I had been raised to play supportive roles to our husbands, never, ever making any attempt to steal the spotlight away from them, even while having our own ambitions.

At that time, I was cautious about Bill Clinton. I thought he seemed a bit smarmy. That now-famous maneuvering of his bottom lip looked to me like a sneer. It took a lot more time for me to notice the man's irrefutable brilliance. By the time of the election, I gladly cast my vote for handsome Bill and returned to my life of ignoring much of political discourse while holding down a junior executive position in a huge corporation . . . until Monica Lewinsky broke through my political unconsciousness.

Despite the glee with which Bill Clinton's adversaries jumped on his boneheaded indiscretion in the Oval Office—something I would ordinarily respond to with loyal defensiveness—I was appalled by the president's stupidity. For me, the honeymoon with Our Bill, as well as Hillary, was over.

I don't call myself a feminist now and I didn't then, but I was fully on board the Women's Liberation train. I make that distinction now because the term "feminist" has taken on a man-hating connotation in some quarters. I love men. I like having them around. I like having discussions with them (even better, sometimes, than I do with women). I just don't want them keeping me down, and I DO want them to pull their weight in relationships. No special treatment. No allowances for testosterone-driven indiscretions. That particular offense had ruined my happy home one too many times, and I developed zero tolerance for it.

When it became clear that Hillary was willing to stand dutifully beside Bill after he disgraced himself and his family by acting like a horny teenager, I realized that she had an agenda that had little to do with wifely duties. And in order to make that agenda come to fruition, she was willing to play a phony role in public, helping her notoriously womanizing mate suffer the impeachment storm intact. I found that off-putting.

As in all things, time healed that wound. Maybe it was because by 2008 I had lived enough of real life to understand the widespread imperfection of human beings. Maybe by then I understood that a person's motive for seeking a goal was less important than what that person brings to the table.

Whatever the reason, I had long since forgiven Hillary enough to fully endorse her first run for the White House. It was time for this bright and tough woman to make history, not *because* she was a woman, but because she was a woman who was supremely qualified to lead a nation.

And then, along came Barack Obama.

I was awestruck by Obama's speech at the 2004 Democratic National Convention. I said that evening, sitting there on my sofa, to whomever was sitting there with me, that I thought we were looking at a future POTUS. But by *future*, I didn't envision the *near* future.

Suddenly, I had a dilemma. Was it more important to support someone who could become the first woman president or the first black president? No matter how hard I tried to be objective by comparing Hillary and Barack solely on the basis of their relative skills and experience, I found myself leaning toward Obama. As a mixed-race woman who is considered black in America, I was suddenly faced with a moveable feast of new possibilities. The idea that a mixed-race man who is considered black in America could occupy the very house in Washington, D.C., that was built by slaves was too intoxicating to dismiss. I have never regretted voting for Obama.

Today, there is no Democrat who can touch Hillary Clinton when it comes to experience. Many people thought of her as a co-president during the Clinton administration; the secretary of state post is clearly in the major leagues of government, not to mention her terms as a U. S. senator. Her work with the Clinton Global Initiative, convening global leaders to create and implement innovative solutions to the world's most pressing challenges, gives her a knowledge of world politics beyond the reach of any candidate in the large group of Republican hopefuls.

Hillary is three years younger than I am. Even though we are of the same baby boom generation, if I'm honest with myself, I am far more politically inspired by people like Elizabeth Warren and Bernie Sanders than I am by Ms. Clinton. They are saying the things I feel are important to the future success of the country. They are talking specifics about the economy, the middle class, and the role of government. They come down hard on the corporation-driven "political dynasties."

But I have learned a thing or two during the Obama years.

I've learned how the government *really* works, and it has little to do with governance and almost everything to do with gaining or preserving power. The ability for the legislative and/or judicial branches of the government to obstruct any and all promises made by candidates has become abundantly clear during the Obama administration. While there is no reason for us to believe that the same phenomenon won't be at play in a Hillary Clinton presidency, she at least has the battle scars she collected from the opposition, and, more importantly, the education she received while collecting them.

My old eyes no longer have stars in them when it comes to politics, but they are wide open. I will not be tempted by the words of Warren and Sanders, no matter how much music they make in my ears. We need a seasoned warrior in the White House. We need someone who will stand in front of a Senate Committee, as Hillary did after the events in Benghazi, and yell, "What difference does it make!?!" Is she as beholden to the controlling corporate puppeteers as the Republicans? Probably.

Is she a bit more hawkish than Warren and Sanders, the two Democrats who suit me more ideologically? Yes, or so it seems, if her past positions can predict the future. That worries me more than a little, but of all the other presidential hopefuls, she is the one who has the experience of balancing her baby boomer ideals, such as the distribution of wealth and the support by the masses for the common good of the nation; Hillary is the only one who understands how to work her ideological agenda within the brutal realities of global government.

Hillary Rodham Clinton is who the United States of America needs in 2016. It will take a career politician with her chops to stop the right wing's efforts to revert to the exclusionary and class-driven policies of pre-FDR America. I am thrilled by the fact that the person who has those qualifications is a woman. Her time has come, and she comes at a crucial time in our nation's history. That's why Hillary Rodham Clinton will get my vote in 2016.

Acknowledgments

For years, I've pondered the question this book set out to explore—what is it with Americans and Hillary Clinton? I could never put my finger exactly on what it was about her in any of the different roles she had since her girlhood days in Illinois that caused so much anger in some people and total devotion in others. Her life—personal, professional, and political—has been on full display for all voters for well over twenty years, and as a result, it seemed like plenty of us felt that we were entitled to judge her and her choices in a way we would almost never do with anyone else.

I knew exploring this question wasn't something I could easily do myself. I knew I would need the minds, wit, and savvy of many other women whose views about politics in general, and Hillary in particular, fell across the full spectrum of varying ideas and life experiences. I particularly wanted women to weigh in on Hillary for this project for two reasons: (1) women voters have decided most presidential elections for the past thirty years, and (2) women writers get significantly less op-ed space than men.

It was an amazing process to collaborate with all the contributors to this book, working through what their individual attitudes were toward Hillary, coming up with the ideas for the essay topics, and watching how each writer developed a particular theme to focus on.

Obviously, this book would not have been possible without all the amazing contributors who graciously gave their time to the writing and editing process, and I am grateful to all of them for wanting to be part of this book, which I do hope will lead us to more fully examine not just our various feelings about Hillary Clinton, but also how we look at and judge all women who decide to run for elective office, and how they are treated by voters and media in way that is vastly different from men. I am so grateful for their work, as well as their excitement, on this project.

Big thanks to my colleagues at *The Broad Side*, a good number of whom contributed pieces for this book. They were more than willing to brainstorm about essay topics and the book's title, they helped to edit my writing as I was editing theirs, and they stepped up to take on additional responsibilities at *The Broad Side* when I had book deadlines. I am so happy and grateful for their support and friendship. A special thanks to Jennifer Hall Lee for the inspiration for the book's title, and to Lisa Solod and Suzi Parker for editing the book's introduction as well as my own Hillary essay as I was editing those of the other contributors. And big hugs and thanks to contributors Anne Born, Linda Lowen, Lisa Solod, and Aliza Worthington for lending exra pairs of eyes in the proofreading process.

This project would not have been possible without Kamy Wicoff and Brooke Warner of She Writes Press. When I had the idea for this book, I sent a note to Kamy to see if they'd be interested in working with me. When I didn't hear back, I assumed the answer was no. Several months later I got a note from Kamy saying, "*Please* tell me I responded to this note!" She put me in touch with Brooke right away, and we were off to the races. As people often say, better late than never! Both Kamy and Brooke, as well as everyone at She Writes, have been so helpful and supportive throughout the process, and convinced me that, yes, it was possible to go from idea to final product in one year!

When I first approached Laura Rossi about being my publicist for this book, she responded immediately with an enthusiastic "yes!" She immediately saw the potential for *Love Her, Love Her Not* to truly jump-start a new conversation about Hillary Clinton as we guessed, rightly (thank goodness!), that she was going to make a second run at the White House. Most of us probably thought we already knew everything there was to know about her, but Laura saw that *LHLHN* would really help us think in new and different ways about Hillary as each of us make up our minds about voting for her or not. I can't thank Laura enough for her amazing ideas, energy, commitment, and resolve.

And, of course, I thank my family so much, for bearing with me through the book writing process which, as writers of any kind know, can often times be difficult and stressful, even when you have huge excitement and a high level of commitment to the project. My husband David and my daughter Rachel hung in there with me as I worked on the research and writing of the introduction, as well my own essay, and gave me the time and space I needed to fully commit to being a good editor to all the other writers.

My daughter Rachel also deserves some extra thanks. As a new high school student who loves writing and the writing process (so much so that she has "threatened" that she might want to get a PhD in English!), she read various drafts of the introduction for me and reminded me that I should loosen up and feel free to write with a little more "sass." It was exactly the right advice at the moment when I needed it.

Here's hoping that whether it is Hillary Clinton or another candidate in the future, I will get to experience the election of a woman to the White House in my lifetime, and that I'll be able to share that with my daughter.

Author Biographies

Veronica I. Arreola is a professional feminist, writer, and mom. Her blog, *Viva la Feminista*, has been named a top political blog by BlogHer, the Women's Media Center and LATISM. Veronica's work on behalf of women and girls has been recognized with a UIC Woman of the Year award, a Chicago Foundation for Women Impact Award, and by the White House with an organizational Presidential Award for Excellence in Science, Mathematics and Engineering Mentoring. Her writing has appeared in *Bitch*, *Ms.*, *USA Today*, and the *Christian Science Monitor*. She lives in Chicago with her husband, daughter, and two rescue dogs.

Lezlie Bishop is a mixed-race Midwesterner who has lived for long periods on both ends of the United States: the San Francisco Bay Area and Atlanta. She retired from a 25-year career with AT&T at age 55, ran her own consulting business for a time, and now spends her days blogging and teaching a class on racism at her local senior center. She, along with three others, published a book in 2014 called *Talking to the Wall*, a dialogue-based discussion of race from both sides of the argument. Lezlie is from the post-WWII generation of baby boomers.

Anne Born is the author of *A Marshmallow on the Bus* and *Prayer Beads on the Train*—collections of stories written on the

MTA. Her blog posts have appeared on *Red Room, Open Salon*, and as a feature in Non-Fiction on *Wattpad*. She is a regular contributing writer on *The Broad Side*. Her writing focuses on family and life in a big city—New York—after growing up in a small one in Michigan. Anne is also a performing artist in the Platform Series at the New York Transit Museum. Follow Anne Born on Twitter and Instagram at @nilesite.

Kim Cottrell is an educator, writer, and retired speech pathologist who has helped countless men and women live more comfortably by improving resilience, posture, and self-image. Since 2009, Kim has blogged at ahealthystepmother.com and is currently writing a book of tales for stepmothers, exposing and questioning the cultural narrative. Kim lives and works in Portland, Oregon.

Mary C. Curtis is an award-winning multimedia journalist based in Charlotte, North Carolina, whose work on politics, culture, and race has appeared in *The New York Times, The Washington Post, The Root, NPR,* and Women's Media Center. She is a political contributor at WCCB Charlotte, and has worked at *The New York Times, Baltimore Sun, Charlotte Observer,* and as national correspondent for *AOL's Politics Daily*. She was a Nieman Fellow at Harvard University and is a senior facilitator at The OpEd Project at Yale University and Ford Foundation. Among her honors are awards from the Association for Women in Communications and National Association of Black Journalists. You can find Mary at www.maryccurtis.com.

Patricia (Tricia) DeGennaro is a geopolitical advisor for the U.S. Army and a professor of international security at New York University's Department of International Affairs. She recently completed a Franklin Fellowship at the United States Agency for International Development in the Office of Civilian Military

Cooperation. DeGennaro capitalizes on over twenty years of experience as an international security and geopolitical consultant. Her subject matter expertise focuses on Afghanistan, the Middle East, the Arab Gulf States, Pakistan, and Iran. DeGennaro publishes on various international security topics including democracy, nation building, political violence, interagency cooperation, civil-military affairs, and U.S. foreign policy. She is an expert commentator for *CNN, MSNBC, Al Jazeera, Fox News, BBC, RT Television*, and various syndicated radio programs. DeGennaro holds an MBA in International Trade and Finance from George Washington University and an MPA in International Security and Conflict Resolution from Harvard University.

KJ Dell'Antonia is the lead writer and editor of the Motherlode blog at *The New York Times*. She lives in New Hampshire, where she votes in whichever party's primary is most interesting in any given year, because she can.

Estelle Erasmus is an award-winning journalist and former magazine editor in chief. She is a co-author of a best-selling beauty book and a contributor to several anthologies, including *The ASJA Guide to Freelance Writing* and *What Do Mothers Need? Motherhood Activists and Scholars Speak Out on Maternal Empowerment for the Twenty-First Century*. Estelle's writing is syndicated on *The Huffington Post* and *What the Flicka* and can be found on *Brain, Child, The Washington Post, Purple Clover, Marie Claire, Working Mother*, and more. She is a member of the American Society of Journalists and Authors and The American Society of Magazine Editors. Estelle blogs about raising a young daughter in midlife at *Musings on Motherhood & Midlife*.

Amy Ferris is an author, editor, screenwriter, and playwright. Her memoir, *Marrying George Clooney: Confessions From* *a Midlife Crisis*, was adapted into an off-Broadway show in 2012. She has contributed to numerous anthologies, including *He Said What, The Buddha Next Door, The Drinking Diaries, Exit Laughing,* and the anthology *Faith.* She is the editor of the anthology *Shades of Blue: Writers on Depression, Suicide, and Feeling Blue* (2015). She co-edited the anthology *Dancing at the Shame Prom.* She has written everything from young adult novels (*A Greater Goode*), to films (*Funny Valentines* and *Mr. Wonderful*) to television series. She has also been both an editor in chief, and contributing editor/writer at the magazines *Urban Refugee* and *Milford Magazine,* and she contributes regularly to *iPinion Syndicate, The Broad Side,* and *The Manifest-Station.* She co-founded and co-created the writing workshop WOMEN OF OUR WORDS/HERShops.

Jaime Franchi is an award-winning journalist who has been recognized by the New York Press Association, the Fair Media Council, and the Press Club of Long Island, a professional chapter of the Society of Professional Journalists. She is the Executive Editor of Morey Publishing, the parent company of *The Long Island Press* and *Milieu Magazine,* for which she is also a staff writer. Jaime's work can be found in *The New York Times, Huffington Post, Salon,* and *The Broad Side.* She lives on Long Island with her husband Marc and their two children Jacob and Anna.

Nancy Giles has been an on-air contributor to *CBS News Sunday Morning* since 2002, with an Emmy Award and two "Gracies" from the Alliance for Women in Media for her work. Her opinions make her a frequent guest on *MSNBC's Melissa Harris-Perry, Hardball, All In with Chris Hayes,* and *Up with Steve Kornacki.* As an actress on stage and screen, she won a Theatre World Award for her Off-Broadway debut in *Mayor,* was part of the ensemble cast of *China Beach* and the sitcom *Delta,* was the announcer and co-host of *Fox After Breakfast*, and on film had small parts with big directors like Clint Eastwood, Woody Allen, and Penny Marshall. On the radio, she was Jay Thomas' sidekick on his *Morning Show* on Jammin' 105 in NYC, and she was half of the award-winning "Giles & Moriarty" (with CBS News' Erin Moriarty) on WPHT in Philadelphia. Nancy has written four solo shows and is a longtime volunteer with The 52nd Street Project in New York City.

Froma Harrop writes a nationally syndicated column on politics, economics, and culture. Represented by Creators Syndicate, Harrop counts *The Seattle Times, Newsday, Dallas Morning News, Denver Post*, and *RealClearPolitics.com* among her nearly 200 subscribers. Harrop has been a two-time finalist for the Loeb Award for economic commentary. She's been honored by the National Society of Newspaper Columnists and has received five awards from the New England Associated Press News Executives Association. Harrop is a frequent guest on *PBS, MSNBC*, and *NPR*. She has also written for *The New York Times, Harper's Bazaar*, and *Institutional Investor*. Born in New York City, Harrop graduated from New York University. She currently divides her time between New York and Providence, Rhode Island.

Jolie Hunsinger, a veterinarian residing in Northeast Pennsylvania, has always had a love of the written word and is excited for the opportunity to be a contributor to this book. Jolie began writing in middle school as a teen columnist for her local newspaper and continued the hobby through her college days, during which she took several creative writing courses to break up her otherwise science-based curriculum. Jolie is an avid Penn State fan who also enjoys expressing her creativity through baking, scrapbooking, and music.

Helen Jonsen is a communicator with a kaleidoscope career as a broadcast journalist, author, commentator, social media enthusiast, speaker, advocate for girls and women, American with an Aussie connection, New Yorker, and Hudson Valley resident. Her work life has taken her from New York television news to Australia and back again. In recent years, she has held senior positions at *Forbes*, *Working Mother*, and Zazoom Media Group, creating digital content across all platforms. As a mom to four, with three daughters, she hopes to see a qualified woman president in her lifetime.

Faiqa Khan is a writer, educator, and self-described peacemaker. She was co-host and producer of the *Hey! That's My Hummus* podcast, which centered on interfaith discussion topics relating to Judaism and Islam. Her writing is published on her award-winning blog www.Native-Born.com. She has edited and produced various online content relating to politics, religion, and cultural identity. Faiqa currently works as a Montessori teacher in Tennessee.

Sally Kohn is one of the leading progressive voices in America. She is currently a *CNN* contributor and columnist for *The Daily Beast*. Sally was previously a *Fox News* contributor, the motivation for her widely seen TED talk, as well as a regular guest on *MSNBC*. Sally's writing has appeared in *The Washington Post*, *The New York Times*, *New York Magazine*, *More Magazine*, *Reuters*, *USA Today*, *Salon*, *Politico*, *Time*, and many other outlets. Her work has been highlighted by outlets from the *Colbert Report* to *The New York Times* to the *National Review*. In 2014, *Mediaite* listed Sally as one of the top nine rising stars in cable news, and *The Advocate* ranked Sally as the 35th most influential gay person in the media. Sally also works as a communications consultant, providing media training and public speaking coaching to political candidates, corporate executives, and non-profit leaders.

Rebekah Kuschmider is a Washington, D.C.-area writer with a background in non-profit management and advocacy. Her work has been seen at *Babble, Huffington Post, Yahoo Shine, Redbook* online, and *The Broad Side*. She is the creator of the blog *Stay at Home Pundit*.

Jennifer Hall Lee is a filmmaker and writer. Her film, *Feminist: Stories from Women's Liberation*, is an independent film about the women's liberation movement. She is also a contributor to *The Broad Side*. She has worked for many years in Hollywood as a visual effects producer and editor on many films including *Forrest Gump, Ghost, Pirates of the Caribbean 2, Beowolf,* and more. She was named as one of the Global Ambassadors for the Global Media Monitoring Project. She grew up in Atlanta, Georgia, and Staten Island, New York. She graduated from Hampshire College and now lives in Los Angeles, California.

Katherine Reynolds Lewis is a Washington, D.C.-based award-winning independent journalist who covers issues related to work, gender, diversity, parenting, and education. A regular *Fortune* contributor, her byline has also appeared in *Mother Jones, TheAtlantic.com, Bloomberg Businessweek, Money, The New York Times, Parade, Slate, USA Today*'s magazines, the *Washington Post Magazine,* and *Working Mother*. She is active in the Asian American Journalists Association, American Society of Journalists and Authors, Education Writers Association, and Society of Professional Journalists. A graduate of Harvard University, Katherine and her husband Brian are the proud parents of three children.

Linda Lowen is co-host/producer of *Take Care*, an award-winning health and wellness show on WRVO Public Media, an NPR affiliate serving Central and Northern New York. The weekly radio show features the country's leading experts on medicine, health, psychology, and human behavior. The show airs Sunday nights at 6:30 p.m. and can be heard as a podcast through iTunes. From 2007–2013 she was editor/writer/content producer for Women's Issues at About.com, owned by the *New York Times Company*. Under her guidance, *About.com Women's Issues* rose to become the Internet's top-ranked site under the search term "women's issues."

Lisa M. Maatz is a nationally sought-after speaker, writer, and political analyst. As a top lobbyist for the American Association of University Women, she's developed a reputation for her strategic approach to legislation and advocacy at all levels. Maatz leads several coalitions working to advance opportunities for women and girls, including the National Coalition for Women and Girls in Education and the Equal Pay Coalition. Maatz has done similar work for other national feminist organizations and was a legislative aide to U.S. Congresswoman Carolyn Maloney (D-NY). Her grassroots advocacy career began when she was the Executive Director of Turning Point, a battered women's program recognized for excellence by the Ohio Supreme Court. Featured in the book *Secrets of Powerful Women*, Maatz also has a devoted following on Twitter (@LisaMaatz). She is a Phi Beta Kappa graduate of Ohio University and has two master's degrees from Ohio State.

Suzi Parker is an Arkansas-based journalist and author whose work has appeared in *The Economist, The Christian Science Monitor, Town & Country, The Washington Post,* and numerous other national and international publications. For several years during the Clinton Administration, she was a contributor to *US News & World Report*, where she covered the construction of the Clinton Presidential Center from start to finish among many other political stories. She is the author of three books, *Sex in the South: Unbuckling The Bible Belt, 1000 Best Bartender's Recipes,* and *Echo Ellis: Adventures of a Girl Reporter,* her first novel, which was published in December 2014. A lifelong Arkansan, Suzi has covered Bill and Hillary Clinton more times than she can count, beginning in the third grade, when she had to write a report about meeting Bill Clinton on a field trip to the state capitol.

Deb Rox is a Florida-based writer, editor, and business strategist who previously served hard time in non-profit management and state government. Her work has appeared on *BlogHer, The Toast, The Butter,* and *The Broad Side,* among other publications.

Lisa Solod is an award-winning short story writer, novelist, and essayist. Her short stories have won several prizes and have been published in numerous literary journals and anthologies. One of her essays was a "Notable" essay in *Best American Essays (2013),* and two of her novels were shortlisted for major literary prizes. She is the author/editor of *Desire: Women Write About Wanting* (Seal Press) and regularly writes for *The Broad Side.* Her essays will appear in three other anthologies in 2015. She can be found at lisasolod.com.

Lisen Stromberg—Sharon Olds once said, "I was a late bloomer. But anyone who blooms at all, ever, is very lucky." Lisen Stromberg, too, is a late bloomer. After twenty years in marketing and business strategy, she began a second career as a writer. Her work has been published in a variety of media outlets including *The New York Times, Newsweek, Fortune, Salon,* and many others. She has won numerous awards for her writing and is currently working on a book entitled *Work Pause Thrive: Where the Will to Nurture Meets the Drive to Succeed* about the importance of leaning in to the full bloom of one's life. You can learn more about her at www.lisenstromberg.com

Aliza Worthington grew up in Brooklyn, New York, and lives in Baltimore. She began writing in 2009 at the age of 40. Sometimes her writing follows The Seinfeld Model of "no learning, no hugging." Other times it involves lots of both. She writes about life, liberty, and happiness at her (sadly, oft-neglected) blog *The Worthington Post*. Her work also appears in *The Broad Side*, *Salon*, *Purple Clover*, *Catonsville Patch*, *Kveller*, and *Daily Kos* (under the username "Horque.") Her piece for *The Broad Side*, "Leaving Gender at the Door," won a BlogHer Voice of the Year award in 2013. Her essay "Heavy Handed Ode to the Clitoris" also won won a BlogHer VOTY award in 2015.

Emily Zanotti is a Republican political strategist and author. She is a regular contributor to *The American Spectator* and a featured opinion columnist with *The Wall Street Journal*. Her work has appeared across the political spectrum, in *National Review*, *The Daily Caller*, *Slate*, and elsewhere.

About the Author/Editor

Joanne Cronrath Bamberger is an award-winning independent journalist, author, political/media strategist, attorney, and an acknowledged expert on women and new media. She is the publisher and editor in chief of the award-winning digital magazine *The Broad Side*, as well as the former award-winning blog *PunditMom*. Her writing has been published in *The Washington Post, USA Today, The Daily Beast, Politics Daily, CNN,* and *The Huffington Post,* among other outlets, and her political commentary has been featured on *CNN, MSNBC, Fox News, XM POTUS Radio,* and more. Her first book was the Amazon bestseller *Mothers of Intention: How Women and Social Media are Revolutionizing Politics in America.* She was named a Forty Over 40 "disruptor" in 2014 and was awarded the Advocacy Innovator Award in 2013 by *Campaigns and Elections Magazine.* Joanne is on the board of directors of the Association of Opinion Journalists. She lives outside of Washington, D.C. with her husband and teenage daughter. You can also find her at joannebamberger.com.

SELECTED TITLES FROM SHE WRITES PRESS

She Writes Press is an independent publishing company
founded to serve women writers everywhere.
Visit us at www.shewritespress.com.

Dumped: Stories of Women Unfriending Women edited by Nina Gaby
$16.95, 978-1-63152-954-2
Candid, relatable stories by established and emerging women writers about being discarded by someone from whom they expected more: a close female friend.

Her Name Is Kaur: Sikh American Women Write About Love, Courage, and Faith edited by Meeta Kaur $17.95, 978-1-938314-70-4
An eye-opening, multifaceted collection of essays by Sikh American women exploring the concept of love in the context of the modern landscape and influences that shape their lives.

Times They Were A-Changing: Women Remember the '60s & '70s edited by Kate Farrell, Amber Lea Starfire, and Linda Joy Myers
$16.95, 978-1-938314-04-9
Forty-eight powerful stories and poems detailing the breakthrough moments experienced by women during the '60s and '70s.

Transforming Knowledge: Public Talks on Women's Studies, 1976-2011 by Jean Fox O'Barr $19.95, 978-1-938314-48-3
A collection of essays addressing one woman's challenges faced and lessons learned on the path to reframing—and effecting—feminist change.

Renewable: One Woman's Search for Simplicity, Faithfulness, and Hope by Eileen Flanagan $16.95, 978-1-63152-968-9
At age forty-nine, Eileen Flanagan had an aching feeling that she wasn't living up to her youthful ideals or potential, so she started trying to change the world—and in doing so, she found the courage to change her life.

Flip-Flops After Fifty: And Other Thoughts on Aging I Remembered to Write Down by Cindy Eastman $16.95, 978-1-938314-68-1
A collection of frank and funny essays about turning fifty—and all the emotional ups and downs that come with it.